■ **A F T E R   T H E   L A W**

A book series edited by John Brigham and Christine B. Harrington

V I R T U O U S   C I T I Z E N S

D I S R U P T I V E   S U B J E C T S

VIRTUOUS CITIZENS
DISRUPTIVE SUBJECTS

ORDER AND COMPLAINT IN
A NEW ENGLAND COURT

■ BARBARA YNGVESSON

■ ROUTLEDGE   NEW YORK ■ LONDON

Published in 1993 by

Routledge
29 West 35 th Street
New York, NY 10001

Published in Great Britain by

Routledge
11 New Fetter Lane
London EC4P 4EE

Copyright © 1993 by Routledge

Printed in the United States of America on acid free paper

Library of Congress Cataloging-in-Publication Data

Yngvesson, Barbara, 1941–
Virtuous citizens, disruptive subjects : order and complaint in a New England court / by Barbara Yngvesson.
p.   cm.— (After the law)
Includes bibliographical references and index.
ISBN 0-415-90766-7 (cloth : acid-free paper) : —ISBN 0-415-90767-5 (paper : acid-free paper)
1. Criminal justice, Administration of —Massachusetts—History. 2. Criminal justice, Administration of—Social aspects. 3. County courts — Massachusetts—Essex County—History. 4. County courts—Massachusetts—Franklin County—History. 5. Clerks of court—Massachusetts—Essex County—History. 6. Clerks of court— Massachusetts—Franklin County—History.   I. Title. II. Series.
KFM2962.Y64   1993
345.744'05—dc20
[347.44055]
93-9376
CIP

British Library Cataloguing-in-Publication Data also available

To my parents, William and Julia Belton,
and to Sigfrid, Dag, and Finn

There are these two ways of understanding the law, the space between two meanings, and their meeting place.

Carolyn Kay Steedman,
Landscape for a Good Woman, 1987

Power is the ability to take one's place in whatever discourse is essential to action and the right to have one's part matter.

Carolyn G. Heilbrun,
Writing a Woman's Life, 1988

CONTENTS

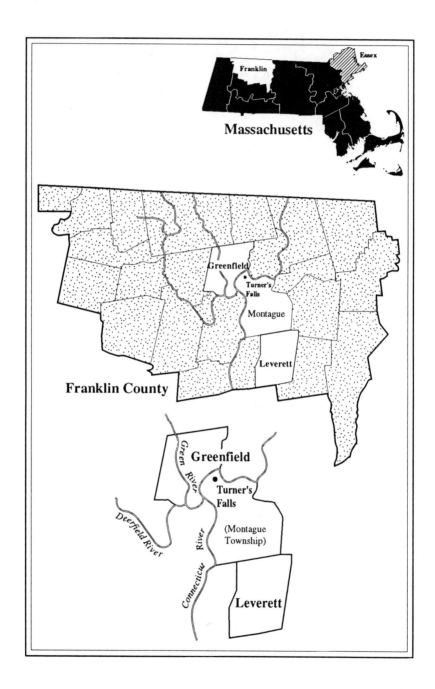

PREFACE

This book is about the power of law and the capacity of court officials and ordinary citizens to transform it. Its subjects are officials who occupy marginal spaces in the legal landscape—district court clerks, lower court judges—and citizens who occupy marginal cultural spaces—"the other half of America," the welfare poor, homeless outpatients of mental institutions. It argues that to understand the power of law, we must examine these borderlands,[1] the encounters with law of those who inhabit them, and how their lives and the law are shaped by these encounters.

To a large extent, the stories told in the following pages are stories of exclusions and of contradictions: a court clerk who is and is not a judge, complaints that are and are not charges of crime, hearings that are held at the courthouse but keep people out of court. These contradictions and exclusions reveal the implicit hierarchies that sustain legal order in the United States; they also point to the spaces where that which is officially defined as *not* law and *not* order continually inserts itself into the law, in a process that both disrupts and reproduces these hierarchies. Neighborhood fights enacted in hearings before a district court clerk are sites where stories of virtuous, self-regulating middle-class lives become standards for distinguishing justiciable complaints from nuisance cases, brought by people with no "moral sense." The law is, in turn, formed in local contests where people without "moral sense" insist on their entitlement to protection from crime.

While the book focuses on the construction of legal order at the margins of official law, I move in the final chapters to a discussion of how order is made by complainants with access to more elite arenas. In superior court hearings, class hierarchies are affirmed in the capacity of more affluent complainants to transform the disorder of complaint into a formal legal appeal. This capacity to harness official law legitimizes their cause, distinguishing it from the local disruptions handled by the court clerk, and affirming their virtue as responsible citizens, entitled to defend and reconstruct public order in court.

ACKNOWLEDGMENTS

This study could not have been carried out without the cooperation and the generosity of court staff in Essex and Franklin counties. I am especially indebted to the court clerks, who were willing to have me or my research assistant sit in on many months of complaint hearings, and to the many citizen participants in the court process who were kind enough to respond to our questions.

My interest in the district court clerk was sparked a decade ago, when Sally Merry suggested that I sit in on complaint hearings held by the clerk at the District Court of Essex in Salem, Massachusetts. She and Susan Silbey were studying a mediation program at that court, and many of the cases that went to mediation were initially seen by the clerk. I commuted for several months to the Salem court, and stimulating discussions with the two of them shaped my early interpretations of clerk's hearings and contributed to my analysis of some of the differences between hearings at the court in Salem and at the court in Franklin County, where most of my research was carried out. In the ensuing years the three of us participated in the Amherst Seminar on Legal Ideology, and I have benefited enormously from the support and the challenge of presenting various incarnations of this work to that group. My first paper on clerk's hearings appeared in an issue of the *Legal Studies Forum* that was collectively edited by the Amherst seminar.[1]

I have also been engaged in three other collaborations that have overlapped in numerous ways with my work on complaint hearings. When I began my fieldwork in Salem, I had just completed several years of research with Lynn Mather on the transformation of disputes. This work provided the theoretical starting point for my study of complaint, and Lynn Mather has continued to be an astute and supportive critic of my work. In a more recent project, together with Maureen Mahoney, who teaches psychology at Hampshire College, I have been working on questions of agency, subjectivity, and social change, and the influence of this joint work has shaped my own understanding of the complaint process and the place of the court clerk in profound ways.[2] Finally, my years of collaboration with

David Engel and Carol Greenhouse on bringing together our separate research on courts in American culture into a co-authored book not only has sustained me (by providing lively comparative discussions on a regular basis), but continually gave me another center from which to rethink my own work and assumptions.[3]

Particular thanks are extended to Randi Silnutzer, first my student at Hampshire College, and then my research assistant for the first 3 years of this project. Her skill as an interviewer and sensitivity as an observer contributed immeasurably to my understanding of the complaint procedure and the meanings of neighborhood conflict in Essex and Franklin counties.

Earlier versions of various chapters of the book have been read by Samuel Bowles, Leonard Glick, Kenneth Kahn, Laurel Kahn, Sally Merry, Alice Rarig, Brooke Thomas, Shirley Thomas, and Austin Sarat. I am appreciative of their patience, tolerance, and good humor, and of their help in sharpening my focus. Christine Harrington and John Brigham provided a detailed critique of the entire manuscript before it was sent to the publisher. I am indebted to them not only for the additional clarity this brought to my project, but also because their commitment and excitement helped me bring it to completion. Finally, I want to thank Maureen Mahoney both for reviewing early chapters and for her careful reading of the completed manuscript. Her insights, enthusiasm and support have been as crucial to this project as to others.

To my families, who have lived with the making of this book for the past ten years, "thanks" does not seem quite enough. But their years of backrubs, encouragement, and willingness to listen to my excitement and my laments are written into every page. I am especially appreciative of my husband Sigfrid's support, and of his capacity, inevitably, to hear what I was trying to say and to help me through the moments when writing seemed most impossible.

My research was supported by a grant from the National Science Foundation (SES 81-22066), as well as by faculty development funds from Hampshire College. Donald Poe generously helped with the statistical analysis of case materials. Pamela Stephan produced the maps for the frontispiece and for Chapter 7. I am grateful to them both for their assistance.

CHAPTER I

INTRODUCTION

STUDYING LOCAL TROUBLE

This project began in a Salem, Massachusetts court in the spring of 1981, and ended on a hilltop in Leverett, the western Massachusetts town where I have lived for the past 21 years. It started as an investigation of the way court officials manage complaints brought to them from local families and neighborhoods, and ended in a neighborhood close to my own, where people I know as friends, colleagues, and acquaintances were involved in a property conflict with the owners of a hill in the center of town. Thus my research moved gradually from the court into the communities surrounding it, and from the more urban east of Massachusetts to the hilltowns of the west, towns with "a long history of independent mindedness"[1] and best known for their involvement in Shay's Rebellion to protest high taxes in 1786.

The project developed out of my research in the late 1970s on the connections of disputing to social order, and specifically on the ways disputes brought to public forums are transformed in the exchanges of official actors (lawyers, third parties, and so forth) with other participants.[2] I was particularly interested in the power of official language to shape the interpretation of events and relationships, and in the ways nonofficial participants in disputing might use established categories in unconventional ways or might create new ones. Research I had carried out several years before on the interpretation and control of conflict in a Swedish fishing village had suggested that the meanings of events as "normal trouble" or as crime emerged over time in the interactions of potential troublemakers and other community members. These interactions redefined collective and individual histories in the context of a single, extended "dispute."[3]

In the Massachusetts study, I was initially interested in how events that were defined by participants as criminal matters were interpreted and transformed by legal officials positioned as "gatekeepers" for the court. I focused both on courthouse struggles over the meaning of everyday events and relationships as normal or serious trouble, and on how events that began as a particular kind of trouble in the neighborhood were transformed into a different kind of trouble for the court itself. Literature on magistrates' and other "lower" courts, as well as on the neighborhood justice movement documented the trivialization and dismissal of neighborhood and family matters by legal officials, who defined them as appropriate for lay mediators but as insufficiently serious for a more formal hearing before a judge.[4]

Two courts were involved in this study of the legal management of local trouble. One is the District Court of Essex in Salem, Massachusetts. The other is the Franklin County District Court, located in Greenfield, in the western part of the state. The comparison of these two institutions suggests how local histories intersect with state power to produce different kinds of local practice. Part of a system of 69 similar institutions throughout the state, "district" or county courts have exclusive territorial jurisdiction over specific villages and towns in the counties where they are located. These courts are the entry point to the court system for the majority of criminal offenses from those areas. District courts handle all misdemeanors except libel, all offenses against local ordinances and bylaws, and felonies punishable by up to 2-1/2 years in a house of correction. The clerk controls access to the court, with discretionary power to allow or deny applications by citizens or by police for the issuance of a warrant or summons. Arrest warrants are issued routinely, typically handled "over the counter" in the clerk's office. Nonarrest complaints by police, and all complaints brought directly by private citizens, are handled in what is known as a "complaint," "show-cause," or simply a "clerk's hearing."[5] In sessions defined officially as preliminary to the criminal process, but resembling courtroom proceedings, the clerk determines whether a complaint application should be issued. This decision shapes the role the court comes to play in a broad range of local conflicts.

I spent 7 months observing over 200 complaint hearings in each of these two courts (March–May 1981 and February–May 1982 in Salem, and June–December 1982 in Franklin County).[6] In addition, I followed complaint applications that were issued as formal charges of crime through other stages of the court process [arraignment, settlement negotiations involving participants and attorneys, trial (if any) and disposition]. At each court, I observed application procedures and informal exchanges involving court personnel, complainants, respondents, and others; and I interviewed judges, attorneys, clerks, probation staff, police, and the parties to complaints.[7] In addition, I conducted docket research on all complaint applications filed with each court during the calendar year 1982, and during March–May 1981 in Salem.

While my research in Salem focused predominantly on the court itself, in western Massachusetts I worked with a research assistant who lived in the town of Greenfield to carry out a more detailed ethnographic study of complaining. This involved following 43 complaints back into the neighborhoods where they began in order to speak with participants and other residents. We also interviewed local police, attorneys, a schoolteacher, reporters for the local newspaper, social workers, an official of the local housing bureau, a landlord, a community organizer, housewives, blue-collar workers, and businessmen. I read the *Greenfield Recorder* (a daily newspaper that covers local events in Franklin County) regularly during 1982–1983, and attended meetings of boards of selectmen, where many local problems are debated.

In exploring the local role of the Franklin County court, I focused on two western Massachusetts towns: Greenfield, a town of 18,400, which is the county seat, and Turners Falls, a community of 4700 people located three miles up the Connecticut River from Greenfield. The contrast in life-style and social organization of these towns illustrates the diverse backgrounds of court users and explains differences in the way court staff respond to complaints and the circumstances from which they emerge. Greenfield, a predominantly working and middle class town of white-collar professionals (lawyers, bankers, doctors, businessmen, state employees) and skilled factory workers, was settled as an agricultural community in the mid-eighteenthth century. Nineteenth century industrialization was concentrated in textile mills and cutlery works, but the failure of some of these and the relocation of others led eventually to the development of the tap and die industry, on which the town's economy was heavily dependent for the next hundred years. Unlike other towns in the Connecticut River Valley, dominated by large-scale industry and characterized by sharp class differences, the tap and die industry in late nineteenth- and early twentieth-century Greenfield was developed in small, locally-owned tool shops and other support industries, and was associated with the enterprise of "native sons" rather than with the wealth of outside investors.

As these Greenfield shops gradually close and relocate today, the interpretation of the past as a local phenomenon shapes fears about an uncertain future in which "outside" capital is associated with moral decline and the deterioration of Greenfield's way of life. Debates about the desirability of attracting new business and fears about undesirable newcomers dominate town politics, are regularly discussed in the media, and emerge in court where cultural, ethnic, and generational conflict is presented in the language of rights and transformed into cases of assault, disturbing the peace, contributing to the delinquency of a minor, and trespassing.

Turners Falls, by contrast, is a more typical milltown. Dominated by tenements once occupied by nineteenth-century factory workers, it has large numbers of unemployed and people on welfare, is the source of most of the clients in Greenfield's numerous social work agencies, and is described by court officials as the residence of "the undesirables" in the county. To Greenfield's middle class residents, Turners Falls is a metaphor for social chaos and the disintegration of what they think of as "community." Yet in Turners Falls the perception of "chaos" is differently constructed and people there, like their more affluent neighbors in Greenfield, use various strategies to control what they perceive as an influx of unwanted outsiders. These include complaining to town government and to local agencies, as well as filing criminal complaints with the court clerk.

This phase of the research, which focused on the courts in Salem and in Franklin County, and on the towns of Greenfield and Turners Falls in western Massachusetts, was completed by the mid-1980s. Shortly after that, in 1987, neighbors in my own town of Leverett became involved in a controversy over the development of a hill that abutted their land, and this conflict was finally taken to the Franklin County Superior Court in 1990. As a resident of the town, I had heard about the controversy, but was not actively engaged in it, and did not attend either the local zoning board hearings or court hearings on the case. However, I conducted long interviews with key participants, and took part in one of the final stages of the controversy. In addition, participants generously made available to me legal and other documents they had collected in pursuing the case.

My engagement with this conflict involved me as both "insider" and "outsider." I know many of its central figures as neighbors, colleagues, or as fellow parents of children at the elementary school, and moved to Leverett as part of the same influx of university and other professionals that brought many of them here, as well. On the other hand, my research in Greenfield and Turners Falls gave me a perspective on the property struggles of Leverett residents that was not shared by people at the center of these struggles; and my familiarity with complaint hearings before the district court clerk provided a vantage point for interpreting the superior court lawsuit brought by Leverett complainants, revealing how "the same" neighbor conflict is transformed by the legal forum in which it is heard. The Leverett case, in turn, provided insights for thinking about complaint hearings in district court, suggesting some of the similarities between the practices of the clerk and the pursuit of a particular vision of order by Leverett complainants. Thus each served as an interpretive context for the other.

The Leverett controversy, like other neighborhood struggles in Greenfield and Turners Falls, revealed the importance of legal complaint to the construction of moral order in the towns of Franklin County. This is partly because of the social meanings attached to going to court for working and middle class citizens;[8] but it is also because the problems defined and brought forward as complaints engage people in "a constant struggle over the criteria for classification, the boundaries of categories, and the definition of ideals that guide the way people behave."[9] These struggles are emotionally powerful engagements in which garbage cases, rights, and crime are discovered in hearings where some complainants constitute themselves as "brainless" by invoking the law, while others become virtuous keepers of community values in court. Engagements such as these catch people up in power relations and in the systems of knowledge they entail.[10]

The principal difference between the Leverett controversy and other Franklin County struggles was in the resources of participants. Parties to the Leverett conflict included professionals and businessmen whose capacity to hire attorneys and file suits in superior court distinguished them from the working class and welfare poor who typically appeared before the district court clerk. The Leverett case thus suggested some of the discontinuities, across class, in the ways local trouble engages the court, while pointing to commonalities in the cultural place of law for everyday citizens. It also allowed me to deepen my understanding of power by exploring how personal, local, and translocal projects intersect, shaping possibilities for action. Examining this intersection was revealing of how power moves people, and of the ways this movement may disrupt, as well as reaffirm, established power relations.

POWER AND THE CONSTRUCTION OF TROUBLE

My focus on the management of trouble as both reaffirming and disrupting power relations draws on three different literatures: work in anthropology, sociology, and history on power and resistance, studies by legal anthropologists of disputing and the negotiation of order, and research by political scientists and others on felony and misdemeanor courts. More specifically, I am interested in the connections between the transformation and crystallization of trouble in courts and other public arenas, on the one hand, and what have been described as "unlikely forms of resistance, subversions rather than largescale collective insurrections, small or local resistances not tied to the overthrow of systems or even to ideologies of emancipation," on the other.[11]

The ambiguity of what Hoebel described as the "trouble case"[12] makes it an ideal focus of research when disputing is understood as a contest about cultural meanings. Both in the Long Hill controversy in Leverett and in complaint hearings before the court clerk, the bearing of neighborhood trouble on the meaning of public order was at the center of the "struggle over ideas" engaging state or town officials and local residents. As the meanings of neighborhood trouble crystallized in public hearings, particular theories of wrongdoing or of virtue were legitimized while others were suppressed, and ideologies of order and of responsibility were reaffirmed and sometimes challenged.

For example, people who appeared repeatedly before the court clerk with complaints of neighborhood fighting both challenged and confirmed official understandings that fighting was part of their "psychology" and that violence was their "way of life." By bringing assault complaints on behalf of their children, complainants insisted on their right to a life that was free of fighting and urged the court to take action that could transform a dangerous neighborhood to a safe one; by issuing their complaints as official charges of crime, the court clerk tacitly acknowledged the legitimacy of their claims. But repeated appearances of the same people in court also contributed to their definition by local officials as "brainless" and unrestrained, and thus in need of official surveillance (if they were not, it was reasoned, they would not depend so regularly on the courthouse for control). Thus complainants confirmed official assumptions that they were incapable of self-control in the very act of claiming rights as citizens.

It is in this sense that recent work examining the connection of subversions or "small" resistances to power is relevant to the cultural interpretation of complaint. Complaints defining violence in poor and transitional neighborhoods as crime, and interpreting safety as a "right," challenge the hierarchies and interests that are embedded in official definitions of trouble; but challenges such as these inevitably implicate people ever more deeply in power relations.[13] The emphasis on subversion as contained by (and productive of) power is an important check on work that romanticizes resistance as evidence of a consciousness that is "outside" of power relations.[14] But it is important as well not to collapse subversion into subjection, obscur-

ing the potential for creativity and invention that is inherent in relations of power.

Work by historian Linda Gordon on the way immigrant women in
nineteenth century America created a "right not to be beaten" focuses
on this potential for creativity in relations of power.[15] Acknowledging
that patterns of class and cultural domination shaped the response
of social workers to complaints of domestic abuse, and that intervention in working class families led to a definition of "rights" that the
victims of domestic abuse "did not always recognize, let alone want,"[16]
Gordon nonetheless argues that complaints by individual victims of
abuse eventually defined women's collective right to freedom from
abuse, and contributed in this way to the transformation of relations
of power over time.[17]

Like Gordon, I am interested in how complaints of violence brought
by poor and working class complainants to state officials may shape
the interpretation of rights. Unlike Gordon, however, who focuses on
the resourcefulness of complainants, my emphasis is on how the invention of rights and the transformation of power is made possible
through the relationship of state officials with parties who complain.
While Gordon notes the creativity of individual social workers in tran-
scending class and cultural bias and the constraints of agency policy,
she mentions their importance in "legitimating [the] . . . complaints
and aspirations" of their clients only in passing and attributes whatever flexibility is reflected in the historical record to "the casework
approach itself," or possibly to an "empathy" by female social workers with their clients.[18] Ultimately, she argues that because social
workers were caught "in a contradictory set of constraints,"[19] their
possibilities for intervention were limited, and they tended to ignore
wife-beating, or defined it as a problem for the victims of abuse to
work on. By contrast, I suggest that it is *because* the court clerk is
caught in a contradictory set of constraints (constraints that tie him,
on the one hand, to parties who complain, and on the other to the
court as "gatekeeper"), that he has the potential for transforming
"local trouble" that is "nothing real vicious" into crime, and for transforming nuisance or "garbage" complaints into rights.

The clerk's manipulation of the "opposing truths"[20] of local trouble
is discussed in detail in chapters 4, 5, and 6. In chapter 5, I examine
how local trial court policy shapes this capacity for maneuver by comparing clerks in the Salem and Greenfield courts, and argue that the
potential for creativity and for subversion through "playing" with
rights is not simply the consequence of aggressive complainants, or of
the occasionally more flexible clerk, but of an interdependence of clerk

and complainants that is forged in historical and contemporary contests. In this way, I suggest the inseparability of subversion and of creativity from established relationships and hierarchies and the connection of complaining to the production of culture. It is *through* his ongoing relations with the citizens who come to him with complaints that the court clerk becomes a "watchdog" for local morality, just as these relationships become the means for local opposition to a legal order in which neighborhood trouble is trivialized and relegated to the "community" or "informal" terrain of law.[21]

DISPUTING AS EMERGENT CULTURE

My approach to complaining as the production of culture builds on work in legal anthropology during the past 20 years in which disputes have come to be seen less as problems in need of a solution than as mechanisms for negotiating and redefining normative order.[22] This shift signaled a reintegration of disputing with politics in a social universe which was seen as "at once rule-governed yet highly negotiable, ordered yet ambiguous."[23]

Legal anthropology in the 1960s and 1970s had moved away from an emphasis on studying law as a structure of rules towards more process-oriented approaches, a development that was shaped in significant ways by the work of Laura Nader and her students in the Berkeley "Comparative Village Law Project."[24] In this move toward process, actors, rather than institutions, became the analytical focus, and disputing tended to displace law as the subject of study.[25] Trouble cases became a vehicle for "extended" or "situational" analysis rather than a means for deriving a corpus of legal rules in societies that lacked statutes or codes.[26] This approach, which embedded disputes in the histories that shaped them, transformed the trouble case into "one phase in the intersecting biographies of the parties concerned"[27] and blurred the boundaries between biography, politics, and law.

The focus on actors and agency directed attention to a broader range of participants in the disputing process (rather than simply to a judge or mediator), as well as examining how rules were manipulated and reinterpreted by participants. Actors were seen as "choosing" between modes of settlement, even as action was described as "channelled" by "constraints and incentives"; and models from game theory were used to explain disputing strategy as actors fought to maximize gains and minimize losses. Even when "maximal loss" was interpreted in noneconomic terms however (that is, as loss of valued relationships), the central figure in processual analyses inevitably reproduced, at the heart of the disputing paradigm, a (western) ratio-nal legal (male) subject.[28]

Subsequent criticism of processual research noted that this literature "assumes too much active-ness" in its emphasis on strategy, calcula-tion, and choice.[29] John Comaroff and Simon Roberts, arguing against the utilitarian bias of much of this research, noted that "[o]nce process is linked with utility—whether utility be conceived in terms of the uni-versalist maximization of interest or the pursuit of indigenous values—it is a short step to treating the sociocultural context as 'given' and its relationship to dispute as unproblematic."[30]

Even as interests seemed to displace rules as implicit motivational forces in the analysis of disputing, attention to what Laura Nader termed the cultural "style" of dispute processes and what Jane Collier described as the "ideology" or "conceptual frameworks" justifying legal action, suggested a more complex reading of agency.[31] "Style" included aesthetic and emotional values, forms of social relations, and the types of cases characteristic of particular economic and political settings as constraints on disputing.[32] Ideology, as Collier used this term, had to do with "culturally available motives for action" as expressed in verbal categories, as people spoke about kinds of wrongs, their motives for quarreling, and acceptable solutions.[33] Both style and ideology required attention to the cultural and social logics through which individual "interests" are experienced and interpreted.

Emphasis on rational pursuit of interests in disputing was also in some tension with the increasing attention given to extended cases. Examined over time, disputing in some relational contexts dissolved into long periods of inaction or "non-action" during which the meanings of particular events as "normal trouble" or as crime were worked out in the context of what was known about an "offender" and his or her sub-sequent actions.[34] Taking this approach, Sally Falk Moore described the emergence of larger political confrontations from individual quarrels in the context of particular kinds of structural oppositions and competi-tions in lineage-based societies; and she noted that an individual offender who was not immediately sanctioned might ultimately be expelled from a group "when his kinsmen are thoroughly fed up with him."[35]

These analyses pointed to the importance of locating the develop-ment of disputes in the history of particular social relations, over time, rather than simply in short-term "interests" and individual choice;[36] and they focused attention on the way historically produced relations of power and inequality shape the emergence of trouble and the capac-ity of actors to name (and even to experience) specific events and relationships as "trouble," as "crime," or as a "dispute" for which remedy might be sought in official or unofficial forums.[37] The tendency of some literature on dispute processes (and of most literature on "dispute processing" by academic lawyers)[38] to abstract disputing from history led some critics to argue that "[t]he attempt to work from the dispute to the social formation is doomed to failure, for the concept of dispute itself is not and cannot be, if so formulated, an *integral* part of a social theory, a theory which should have itself created the space for such a concept."[39]

While this critique was important in pointing to the ideological bias in much of the dispute processing literature, the call for a move away from studies of disputing to research on structural conflict (and the implicit and sometimes explicit trivialization of "interpersonal" quarrels that accompanied this) reproduced the very biases (law/dispute, public/private, structural/personal) of the dispute processing literature itself.[40] By privileging structure over family and neighborhood "quarrels," the critique of studies of dispute implicitly separated power from the "interpersonal" conflicts of everyday life, and risked losing the key insight of processual studies of the 1970s, that "conventional conceptions of social structure serve to make apparently stable, simple order out of very complex, interwoven and continuously shifting relationships."[41]

By examining the connection of the "personal" and the "relational" to the structural, research on disputing can contribute to the analysis of modern mechanisms of power which "seem . . . to stand outside actuality, outside events, outside time, outside community, outside personhood."[42] Timothy Mitchell describes this as "enframing,"[43] in which power (as structure or as culture) appears to be external to practice and imposed on it, rather than continuously at work within the "choices" and everyday struggles of men, women, and children. The analysis of disputes is always an analysis of power relations, as these structure the definition and interpretation of trouble in families, neighborhoods, courts, and in other "private" and "public" settings.[44] Disputing needs to be theorized, but not as an activity distinct from these relations of power. Rather, disputing can be theorized as a form of action-in-the-world in which the connection of the "personal" to the "structural" is both given and emergent, and in which disputes both affirm asymmetries of gender, class, and ethnicity and may challenge these, revealing their openness to contestation.[45]

COURTS AND LOCAL MORALITIES

This work suggests ways for thinking about how courts are shaped through the practices of citizens who use them (and of those who avoid them) while acknowledging the force of law both in making courts and in creating the social world.[46] Literature on lower courts in the United States tends to focus on their insulation from everyday life, specifically through a shared culture in which distinct understandings about the meanings of crime, the meanings of "trouble," and about kinds of troublemakers, set the institution and those who work there apart from those who move through it as victims, as defendants, or as complainants. Studies of court organization and analyses of practices such as plea bargaining describe the exclusion of victims and defendants in the management of cases in court.[47] Nonprofessionals become "outsiders in the courtroom," moved through the system by knowledgeable insiders who *are* the system and shape its contours.[48] For the problems of these victims and defendants to become "cases" in court, they must be framed in legal terms, subjected to official definitions of crime or of "normal trouble,"[49] and turned over to specialists trained in the intricacies of legal argument. The experience of coming to court, whatever the outcome of the complaints that are brought there, is described as disempowering of lay citizens, whose stories must be told in the formulas provided by prosecutors, police, defense attorneys and others who control the development of each case.[50]

Research on felony and misdemeanor courts also points, however, to the dependence of "insiders" in the court on the "outsiders" who move through it on a regular, and often repetitive, basis.[51] Each defines the status of the other, suggesting a more complex portrayal in which it is the ongoing interactions of professionals with lay citizens that constitute "the system." A close examination of these interactions points to the key role they play in reproducing an ideology of law as distant from everyday life and of professional expertise as distinct from common sense knowledge. Indeed, these interactions become a site for the production of different kinds of legal forums, and of distinguishing the central from the marginal in the sphere of law.[52] Police, prosecutors, court clerks, and others patrol the boundaries of law, becoming gatekeepers through their exchanges with victims and other participants in incidents of trouble.

Thus in this study I show that the court is not solely shaped by professionals but that the law, the court, and legal officials are formed in the exchanges of officials with victims, defendants, witnesses, and others about the meanings of the words and actions that bring people to the courthouse. In these exchanges, and in collective practices that develop around them, "cases" and "courts" are constituted, as everyday acts and spaces are transformed into legal ones. This inevitably links the court to the "ways of life" that local communities claim, at the same time that court practices define legal rules and legal forums as domains that are set apart from community.[53]

The place of the Franklin county court as an arena where competing visions of community and of law are enacted emerges from the historical practice of lay magistrates and justices of the peace in colonial New England. The ambiguous place of a "magistraticall authority"[54] tied to local cultural practices, but securely grounded in the power of a small ruling elite, is reconstituted today in the authority of a court clerk who is empowered as much by his local identity and local knowedge as he is by his position as an official of the Commonwealth. The complex identity of this official is central to the place of the court in local politics. Other studies document an ethic of entitlement among working class citizens who seek justice in court, an ethic of virtue among others who avoid the court, or a compartmentalization of social life that allows people to insulate themselves from conflict without resorting to court.[55] The court described in this book is avoided by some and used as an instrument of defamation by others, but both of these practices help make the court a particular kind of institution, shape the law as a particular kind of order, and construct the identities of complainants and others who approach the law or avoid it as agents of a particular kind.

My account, then, moves from an examination of the telling and interpretation of particular tales—of lovers' quarrels, neighborhood antagonisms, family hostilities, and community divisions—to an analysis of why the tales are told in particular ways, of which accounts are privileged and which are silenced, and of how the context of the telling shapes what can be told, who is empowered to make common sense of it, and the moral and legal frameworks that emerge from particular narratives of trouble. This requires attending to the role of local audiences in constructing stories of trouble, and to a "participatory" process (such as mediation or "informal" hearings before a court clerk) that contributes to the reproduction of particular forms of domination. In this way my account locates "law," "court," "cases," and "community" in everyday processes of complaint, conflict, and cooperation. These processes are channeled in particular ways by dominant communal and legal understandings and practices. This approach to the production of law and of trouble acknowledges the complex and unsettled relationship of law to other social forms without collapsing one into the other;[56] and it examines this relationship in the moments of its reproduction, by agents who are both constituted by the law and who confront the law, editing its meanings by their very presence at the court.

ORGANIZATION OF THE BOOK

The second chapter begins with a description of official court policy for handling interpersonal complaints by citizens in show-cause hearings before the court clerk and examines how a legal canon polarizing state and local, legal and interpersonal was shaped as law was professionalized and state power consolidated in postrevolutionary America. The third chapter, "This is Not Coney Island," describes the ideology of community and of local control in Greenfield, and the ambiguous place of the court as a symbol both of state power and of regional autonomy. It discusses the different meanings of complaining for private citizens (who use the complaint procedure to claim entitlement to law, and as a way of empowering themselves by involving the court in neighbor and family struggles) and for court staff, whose ongoing relations with complainants provide them with a basis for "watching" local families and neighborhoods.

The fourth and fifth chapters compare complaint narratives and hearings in Franklin County and in the District Court of Essex in Salem as a way of examining how a tradition of local control in western Massachusetts shapes the more powerful position of the clerk there, as well as providing an arena in which the parties to complaints have space for maneuver. I argue that the power of the clerk (his capacity for governance in the complaint process) is intimately connected to the local meaning of complaining as a way of bringing people to the courthouse while keeping them "out of court," and to the symbolism of the courthouse as a building that stands for local autonomy and identity vis-à-vis the state. At the District Court of Essex in Salem, by contrast, show-cause hearings are marginal procedures, increasingly defined either as "purely administrative" or as appropriate for trained mediators rather than court staff, at an institution that stands as a model for the professional administration of the law of the Commonwealth.

The sixth chapter focuses on the room for maneuver at the Franklin County court by examining a series of complaints from Turners Falls, a neighboring town that is perceived by Greenfield residents as having a "fighting" way of life. By analyzing the tension between dominant and competing meanings in the complaints enacted by Turners Falls residents at the courthouse, I suggest how complaint is both a discourse of resistance and a critical vantage point from which the law can be known.

The seventh chapter moves back to the theme of "watching" by virtuous citizens to examine the use of legal complaint by affluent residents of the Franklin County town of Leverett. As in Chapter 6,

I focus on the contradictions of a discourse of entitlement in which actors are constituted as at the same time self-interested and greedy, and as moral agents working for collective goals. Like the disruptive subjects from Turners Falls in the previous chapter, Leverett property owners both reaffirm and disrupt dominant meanings in struggles at the courthouse that would "save" community through law, even as their legal claims are interpreted as a sign of the demise of local understandings.

In the final chapter, I consider the implications of this analysis in the context of theory that describes resistance as subjection. I argue that the "double reality" of neighborhood struggles at the courthouse is constituted in a play with rights that both enmeshes people in the power of law and reinterprets the law, reproducing hierarchies that distinguish virtuous from disruptive citizens and upper from lower courts, while providing an embedded critique of these hierarchies in the everyday practice of complaint.

CHAPTER 2

"THE CLERK IS LIKE A WATCHDOG . . ."

A justice of the peace is halfway between a man of the world and a magistrate, an administrator and a judge . . . . For that reason his responsibility is only to be society's policeman, a matter requiring good sense and integrity more than knowledge.

When the American people let themselves get intoxicated by their passions or carried away by their ideas, the lawyers apply an almost invisible brake which slows them down and halts them.

Alexis de Tocqueville,
Democracy in America, 1850

NEIGHBORHOOD QUARRELS

Cici Morris marched into the clerk's office at the Franklin County District Court in Greenfield with her two young children and slammed a kitchen knife down on the counter. "Angel Sanchez chased Toby with this," she said. The children, a boy and girl 5 and 6 years old, told the clerk that Angel had chased them, and the little girl had thrown a bottle at him. Then Angel ran after Toby with the knife, they said, and finally threw the knife in the bushes. The clerk listened patiently to this account, letting the children talk without interruption, then called the Turners Falls police to have them look into the incident. He helped Cici to fill out a complaint application for assault, and scheduled a show cause hearing for the following week.

Earlier that same afternoon, Angel's mother, Maria Sanchez, had also filed complaints with the clerk, alleging that Robert Morris, Cici's husband, had assaulted her and that Jack Pulaski, another resident in the Turners Falls tenement where she lived with her four children, had threatened to "crush her face." She was accompanied by her son, 14-year-old Miguel, who stood by in silence while the clerk helped her complete the forms for threats and for assault.

These complaints were part of a series of hostile exchanges involving the Sanchez family and other residents of three neighboring houses on Clapp Street in Turners Falls. The Morris family had bought their house 4 years earlier, and spoke of their concern about the deterioration of the neighborhood once Maria Sanchez and her children moved in. They described the Sanchez children as "unsupervised," and told stories of Maria "staying out until three in the morning." "The state police found her in a bar one night, and had to take her somewhere and sit and feed her coffee, with the four boys at home alone." They had complained to the landlord, to the housing authority, and to the fire department, when the youngest Sanchez child started a fire in a closet. "We own our own home, and when you have a house, and there's kids next door setting fires . . . "

The Sanchez family was one of the first Hispanic families to move to Turners Falls, but the Morris family denied that race was an issue in the hostilities: "They say it's because we're prejudiced. It ain't that! If it was white kids setting fires, we'd feel the same way." The fears voiced by Cici Morris are widely shared in the "downstreet" area of Turners Falls, where residents talk about bad neighbors and owners of small businesses worry that undesirable loiterers will discourage customers. At selectmen's meetings in 1982 and 1983, residents and businessmen crowded the small meeting room to protest construction of a new, low-income housing development in the downstreet area, expressing their apprehension that, in one woman's words, it would be "filled with a lot of Puerto Ricans."[1] Anxiety about unwanted outsiders speaks to a more general unease about the changing face of the town, and emerges in conversations with people of all ages in Turners.

At hearings scheduled for these and related complaints, the clerk interpreted the hostilities as "problems with children" and spoke with complainants about parents becoming involved in children's fights. Describing some of the incidents as "nothing real vicious," the clerk issued two of the complaints "technically" but "held" them "at the show cause level."[2] Two other charges were acknowledged as more serious, and these matters were scheduled for arraignment in court. Subsequently, these too were dismissed, after a period in which they were "continued without a finding."[3]

In Greenfield, Cheryl Roche filed a complaint with the clerk for disturbing the peace, complaining that her next door neighbors, an elderly couple and old time residents of the town, screamed profanities at her children and called the Roches "scum from Springfield."[4] The elderly couple objected to the children playing with their Big-Wheels toy on the sidewalk in front of their home, and sent their grandson out on *his* Big-Wheels to smash into the Roche child's toy. "I went back into the house and called the police. They came and were talking to them for about 20 minutes . . . . Then he said something like 'God damn it' . . . . We'd warned them about three or four times not to use profanity. They're also always calling us 'scum'. I don't think that's right." The older residents complained about the noise created by the Roche children: "After a while, that noise gets to you, and I told them to play in front of their house . . . . Then, I called the police. It's the constant noise of those things after a while. In 42 years in that house, I've had no problems to speak of. My mother brought me up being in business—that you have to be better neighbors." The clerk suggested to the Roches that "there's degrees of swearing"; and he pointed out to the older residents that "you do have to realize it's 1982 . . . . [A]nybody who wants to use that sidewalk has a right."

These complaints are typical neighbor conflicts brought by private citizens to the district court clerk in Franklin County. Framed as problems of noise, of profanity, or of threat, they are experienced as infringements of legal entitlements to peace, to physical protection, and to social space. As in other neighbor conflicts, the local police or other officials were called a number of times before the neighbors appeared at the courthouse.[5] When their intervention did not resolve the problem, police advised the complainants to file an application for a criminal complaint with the clerk, and ultimately the parties appeared in a "show cause" or "complaint hearing" before him.

This hearing, required by Massachusetts law for all complaints of a misdemeanor brought by citizens or by police, is the first step in initiating criminal proceedings in cases where there has not been an arrest.[6] Described officially as a protection for the person against whom the complaint is sought, the show cause hearing permits her "an opportunity to be heard personally or by counsel in opposition to the issuance of any process based on such complaint."[7] More significantly, however, the hearing is viewed in trial court policy and in local court practice as a way of settling local conflicts informally in proceedings that attend to "community values" rather than to individual rights or questions of law.[8]

Citizen complaints, in particular, are regarded as out of place at the court. They are generally viewed by criminal court officials in this country as "garbage" cases, and in Massachusetts, the clerk is urged in the trial court's *Standards of Judicial Practice* to "refrain from initiating criminal proceedings [in these cases] where the conflict can be fairly resolved by something less."[9] As the Clerk Magistrate in Greenfield noted:

> People must be educated to what courts can do, and to what courts *can't* do. People must be educated that the *court* has some limitations . . . . The court can sanction, so people want it to resolve all manner of conflicts.

A "garbage case," in the language of court officials, describes "everyday" conflict, a "shoving match in which somebody threw the first punch," "kids pushing kids," or a "lover's quarrel," but the term includes a broad range of conflicts in the family, the neighborhood, or the workplace. Complainants arrive at the courthouse "in the heat of the moment," and (in the view of court staff) need a "referee," a sounding board, or advice.[10] Initial screening of these complaints in the neighborhood by police points to their subsequent definition as "garbage" at the court, where two-thirds are dismissed by the clerk or withdrawn by the complainant before, during, or after a show cause hearing. This means that while people are permitted, and in some jurisdictions encouraged, to "come to the courthouse," few of their complaints result in the issuance of a formal charge of crime (Table 2.1).[11]

Table 2.1. Disposition of Complaints Filed by Private Citizens and by Police in Franklin County, June 1–December 31, 1982

Outcome	% (Number) of Complaints Brought by Police	% (Number) of Complaints by Private Citizens
Allowed	82% (265)	33% (96)
Denied	8% (26)	31% (92)
Withdrawn	5% (15)	24% (71)
Continued	5% (14)	12% (34)
Total	100% (324)	100% (293)
Total Complaints by Citizens and Police: 617		

Withdrawal by a complainant and denial by the clerk are sometimes hard to distinguish. Almost half of the 71 withdrawals (48%) occurred during or after the hearing; in the hearings I observed, many of these resulted from efforts by the clerk to mediate a conflict.

Dismissal of citizen complaints by the clerk should not be confused with disengagement, however. Dismissal strategies involve numerous techniques that allow the court to continue monitoring cases that are officially denied, including "technical issuance," continuing a case "for a few months to see if there is any more trouble," and "holding a case at the show cause level."[12] Monitoring of this kind identifies the court as a place dominated by the problems of irrational people who "just don't *want* to get along" (in the words of an Assistant Clerk), and keep coming back. This identity persists even as dismissals of citizen complaints constitute the court as a place where "garbage cases" are excluded so serious problems of order can be dealt with. "Technical" issuance officially legitimates the entitlement of citizens to "be heard" while keeping them out of court; but it also transforms problems that "will never be solved" into cases that "won't go away." Such cases comprise almost as much of the court's work as the criminal charges by which its official business is measured, and define the clerk's role as both court and community "watchdog."[13]

Complaints brought by the police to the clerk are interpreted and handled quite differently than those brought by citizens. Most are allowed, and few are given a hearing. Of 617 complaints filed with the Franklin County clerk between June and December, 1982, 324 were brought by police, and 82% (265) of these were allowed, compared with 33% of the complaints brought by private citizens (see Table 2.1). Indeed, most police complaints are allowed "over the counter" at filing, without a show cause hearing (Table 2.2).

Table 2.2. Complaints That Led to Hearing versus
Those Allowed without a Hearing, by Type of Complainant

Disposition of Complaint	% (Number) of Complaints Brought by Police	% (Number) of Complaints by Private Citizens
Allowed w/o a hearing	56% (183)	11% (32)
Led to a hearing	39% (127)	77% (227)
Undetermined hearing status	4% (14)	12% (34)
Total	100% (324)	100% (293)

When a hearing is conducted, however, assumptions about the seriousness of the trouble and its implications for public order differ markedly from those in complaints by private citizens. The following case illustrates this difference.

"YOU CAN'T SHORT-CUT THE LAW"

A Greenfield policeman filed a complaint with the clerk for the "deliberate and malicious" damage of a maple tree on Shady Lane. The tree bordered the street and was the property of the town. The police went to the clerk after receiving a complaint from the Department of Public Works (DPW) that the owner of the house in front of which the tree was growing had "girdled" the tree by cutting the bark all the way around it so that it would die. The DPW had sent a $257.76 bill to the owner (Joe Graham) for the cost of removing the tree. When Graham refused to pay the bill, the DPW complained to the police.

There was no dispute about who had damaged the tree. Graham, a young man who described himself as "in the tree-cutting business," admitted girdling the tree because it was damaging his sewer and was dangerous to passersby. He claimed that it had almost fallen on a neighborhood child. He explained that the Board of Selectmen in Greenfield had denied his request to have the tree removed a year and a half earlier, but that one of the selectmen had said he could remove the tree himself if he wished. Asked about this by the police, the selectmen confirmed that Graham had asked them to remove the tree, but denied that they had suggested he cut the tree down himself. The police then tried to negotiate the cost of removing the tree with Graham and when they were unsuccessful, brought the complaint to the clerk.

At the hearing, Graham explained that he could not afford the bill for removing the tree because he was already in debt to his father. He added:

> As far as malicious cutting of the tree . . . especially given a five year-old kid that almost got killed . . . it's certainly not malicious. [And he explained:] They've got a telephone line going right through the center of it. They cut out the entire center, but they didn't paint it. So the limbs are just falling off. We tried that chemical [used for killing roots in the sewer] . . . Right now, we've got the sewer open, we have to! Every time it rains, we have a flood in our basement. The town came to clean up from the fallen limb, and the guy says, if it gets into the main sewer line, they'll have to dig up the whole road at my expense . . . . It's a small tree. One person could take that tree down. I said, I'll gladly take it down. . . . We've got toilet paper and everything going right down into our cellar.

The clerk, who described this as a "catch 22 situation," noted to the policeman that issuance of a complaint would give the man a criminal record, even if he ultimately did not have to pay the fine. The policeman maintained, however, that the head of the tree crew at the Department of Public Works wanted to "push this thing through." The clerk continued the complaint for a week to see if something could not be worked out by the police, the DPW, and Graham. He explained to Graham: "This could be a principle thing. They could be afraid that if you get away with it, everybody will be doing it. In that case, you'll just have to go to court and let the judge decide." In the end, that is what happened. The clerk issued the complaint and the court ordered Graham to pay restitution to the town.

The policeman who handled this complaint explained that his aim was to show Graham that he couldn't short-cut the law: "He knew exactly what he was doing! If he thought he could get away with it he would have cut the tree right down." And he noted that the clerk "*had to issue it. . . . Just look at [chapter] 2666-113A, that's all. . . . If you really want to, you can find a law to do what you want to do*" [emphasis added]. The young man's reaction to the decision was that the DPW, the police, and the court all work together and "You can't fight 'em. They'll get you if they want to."

INTERPRETIVE COMMUNITIES AND THE CRYSTALLIZATION OF TROUBLE

This complaint illustrates the difference between a "neighborhood disturbance" that is "nothing real vicious" (in the view of court officials and police) and disorder that police and the court ultimately get involved with. The clerk agreed that the tree was a hazard: "it was a bad tree." But he argued that Graham should have gone beyond the selectmen in bringing it to the attention of the town. "He should have had the mother of the child raise a fuss, and have had the newspaper pick up on it. Then the town would have *had* to act." "The town," temporarily mobilized by petitions to the selectmen and letters in the daily paper, could transform a situation that was defined officially as a local nuisance (a man complaining about a tree) into a public danger (a tree threatening passersby); this, in turn, would determine the "need" for official (police) protection, and would give local citizens some say in what this protection should consist in. This view comes from the clerk's understanding of the different ways that "hazard" might be constructed by different audiences in the community and the strategies for controlling the meaning of events such as this one.

In this case, Graham's complaints to the town were transformed from nuisance into hazard when he girdled the tree; but for police and

DPW officials, it was *Graham*, and not the tree, who constituted the hazard. He had acted against a decision by the selectmen. On his own, he had chosen to destroy town property publicly, setting in question the official role of the Department of Public Works to protect and maintain it; and he refused to cooperate with police efforts to negotiate a settlement. Thus it became "a principle thing" for police and the town.

The "girdled tree" illustrates a theory of trouble as "the emergent product, as well as the initial precipitant, of remedial actions"[14] and shows how trouble "crystallizes" as it moves through a series of troubleshooters to become "a case."[15] The mobilization (or potential mobilization) of different relevant audiences shaped the meaning of the damaged tree for the town, of what or who constituted hazard, and of what was required to protect "the community" in this complaint.[16] Thus, it brings into relief the layers of meaning in which local events are embedded, and the power of state agents such as the police to impose an "official truth" on these events.[17]

Not only does the case of the "girdled tree" say something about how different interpretive communities construct sociolegal life, but it highlights the importance of property in official conceptions of crime. In general, complaints brought by Franklin County police to the clerk tend to be framed as offenses against property (Table 2.3) and these complaints may receive official recognition through issuance as formal criminal charges by the clerk (see Table 2.1). By contrast, private citizens frame complaints to the clerk as offenses against the person (Table 2.3), and most of these are dismissed (see Table 2.1), or are "continued without a finding" by the court, as in the case involving Angel Sanchez and the knife, described above.

Table 2.3. Type of Offense by Type of Complainant, Franklin County, June 1–December 31, 1982.

Type of Offense	% (Number) of Complaints by Police	% (Number) of Complaints by Private Citizens
Property offense	59% (190)	33% (97)
Offense against the person	16% (53)	58% (170)
Victimless	18% (57)	4% (11)
No information on type of offense	7% (24)	5% (15)
Total	100% (324)	100% (293)

This apparent difference between police and citizen complaints must be interpreted in light of police involvement in sifting trouble in the family and neighborhood before it is taken to court, and specifically in terms of their role in recommending that citizens go directly to the clerk with complaints, when the police are unwilling to make an arrest.[18] The framing of citizen complaints as assaults, threats, disturbing the peace, and the like occurs in the context of exchanges with a series of official troubleshooters, including the police and the clerk, and the interpretation of these complaints as "interpersonal" rather than property matters emerges through these exchanges.[19]

Yet the details of neighborhood trouble presented in complaint hearings suggest that "assaults" and "threats" inevitably occur in connection with experiences of property transgression ("trespassing"), property damage ("malicious destruction"), or a "right" to peace (for example, in charges of neighborhood noise) by those involved.[20] While damage claims, in particular, may provide a basis for the clerk's efforts to settle a complaint, these and other property claims by citizens are excluded from official interpretations of what neighborhood trouble is about.[21]

This is related, in part, to differences in the way court officials and citizens understand property rights;[22] but the question whether neighborhood trouble should be defined officially as property transgression or as feud (people who "can't live together and can't live apart," in the words of one court clerk) depends on *who* the "feuding" parties are (trouble between the DPW and a private citizen is not a feud), and on having "the capital of authority necessary to impose a definition of the situation."[23] In this way, "'egoistic,' private, particular interests (notions definable only within the relationship between a social unit and the encompassing social unit at a higher level) [can be converted] into disinterested, collective, publicly avowable, legitimate interests."[24] The clerk's capacity to do this is constrained by his official mandate as magistrate for local (that is, "private") matters, and by trial court policy and practice.[25] The personal *belongs* before the clerk, a local magistrate for whom formal legal training is not required; by contrast, property crime, a threat to "the material foundation of both personality and government,"[26] is the responsibility of police, who bring official charges of crime in court. Citizens who possess the resources to go beyond local officials and involve the superior court in a neighborhood struggle may be able to transform "interpersonal" trouble into property trouble, however.[27] Because property ownership and property transgression have such powerful connections with the definition of self in American culture,[28] this transformation may be important in engaging a broader audience with the case.

Seen in this light, complaint hearings reveal some of the dimensions of what Boaventura Santos terms "interlegality." Interlegality means that sociolegal life is "constituted by different legal spaces operating simultaneously on different scales and from different interpretive standpoints."[29] Legal officials may use the hearings to "manipulate legal aspirations—to create them in certain cases, to amplify or discourage them in others,"[30] as could be seen in the exchanges of the court clerk with Graham in the "girdled tree." But the hearings are also a legal arena where different interpretive standpoints intersect as clerk, local citizens, attorneys, and other officials come together to argue and negotiate a broad range of family, neighbor, and town problems. Conventional meanings of everyday events are named, debated, made reasonable, and sometimes resisted in these engagements, which are at the same time spaces where law makes the social world[31] and sites where the arbitrariness of this world may be revealed.

The clerk's more complex interpretation of hazard in the "girdled tree," even as he prepared to issue the complaint demanded by the DPW, suggests the complexity of his position in a world where official and unofficial truths coexist, and where the clerk occupies the potential space between these different truths.[32]

THE EMERGENCE OF LAY JUSTICE

The designation of court clerk as the magistrate for local problems in Massachusetts today is the outgrowth of a long history of struggle over the role of the legal profession in the administration of justice, and more generally over the place of lawyers in the governance and transformation of social order. In the colonial period, nonlawyer judges were key figures in local governance through their position as "peace-keepers" in colonial sessions courts.[33] "Keeping the peace" in seventeenth- and eighteenth-century New England referred in a broad way to local governance, and included what today would be distinguished as criminal and civil functions of the court, as well as administrative regulation. Sessions courts handled sexual and other moral offenses, offenses against the peace (e.g., "Mutinous and Riotous Behavior"), defamation, and offenses against property, as well as complaints of debt or of trespass.[34] They also distributed and regulated liquor licenses, were key players in empowering towns to decide who would receive poor relief and who would be "warned out," and enforced the maintenance of county roads.[35] In the first half of the eighteenth century, the court was "an institution of undifferentiated local government authority . . . [and] made a single continuum of judicial action out of the disparate forms of criminal and administrative business that came before it, a continuum which made possible a judicial government of county life."[36]

In colonial America, judicial governance, like English local government from which it derived, was in the hands of local gentry, who were given broad discretionary power both in what they chose to hear and in how they allocated punishments.[37] At the same time, the control of magistrates over peacekeeping was dependent on the willingness of aggrieved parties to bring conflict to court. Because of this, eighteenth-century sessions courts developed encouragements to criminal litigants and litigation, permitting the use of law "as a kind of weapon" for "instrumental accusations" so that judges could "enforce a complex vision of the good moral order of the county."[38]

The relationship of judge to citizen changed in the postrevolutionary period, when the governance and criminal functions of sessions courts were separated. In a move that would transform what was widely regarded as a cumbersome and oppressive judicial system, the criminal jurisdiction of the courts was gradually integrated into a state-wide system of criminal justice.[39] This process culminated with the Progressive reforms of the early twentieth century, eroding the power of lay magistrates who were gradually moved into peripheral roles in "inferior" courts or eliminated altogether.[40] Similarly, the centrality of local conflict to the peacekeeping activities of courts came into question. Rather than "an instrument as well as an instance of local government authority," these conflicts were defined as the "everyday" quarrels of "irrational" people and placed in the hands of gatekeepers whose job was to keep them *out* of court. Only if defined as "a lesser form of felony case" could they be viewed as suitable business for the law.[41]

Lay judges and everyday citizens were also marginalized with the emergence and consolidation of a powerful legal elite in the new American republic. This process began just after the Revolution and continued, with considerable resistance, during the first decades of the the nineteenth century.[42] Resistance to a professional elite was particularly intense in Massachusetts, where the debate over judicial reform was linked to demands to abolish the legal profession and to a more radical politics supporting the rights of agrarian over commercial interests.[43] This resistance culminated in Shay's Rebellion (1786), when impoverished farmers in the Berkshire Hills and Connecticut valley marched with guns and pitchforks to prevent the county courts from sitting to judge debt cases. At one point, much of Hampshire and Berkshire counties and parts of Middlesex and Worcester counties were controlled by rebel forces.[44]

Opposition of this kind produced some reforms that constrained the power of the bar, but this temporary setback to professional power was shortlived. Allied with increasingly powerful commercial interests, elite lawyers interpreted their mandate ever more broadly as "a popular charter to mold legal doctrine according to broad conceptions of public policy,"[45] rather than as a vehicle for local governance. Indeed, it was in this process that "local disputes" were increasingly distanced from public policy, while policy was formed through the relationships of elite lawyers with business clients whose practice was shaping a translocal market. This emerging translocal community of professionals could be seen throughout Massachusetts, where lawyers and businessmen in Greenfield, as well as in Boston, were increasingly involved in collaborative enterprises to broaden the transportation network connecting western settlements to coastal towns and beyond.[46] In Greenfield, the transformation of the town into a regional marketing and transportation center became the basis for its designation as "shire town" of the new Franklin County in 1811, and as the seat for the county court.[47]

Transformations such as these both enhanced local identifications and redefined the meaning of these identifications.[48] The "local" and the "lay" were constituted as "personal" and "low," a hierarchy of value that emerged in conjunction with differences of class and of culture in the relations of native and immigrant populations in nineteenth-century America. The change in legal culture also produced a "high culture" of a white, largely Protestant, male, legally trained professional elite and a "low culture" of locally based order-maintenance officials.[49] In the view of elite lawyers and reformers, local practices and values were compromised by "personal" relationships, while professional practices were seen as "emotionally detached,"[50] the product of "trained minds . . . free from interest or bias."[51] Lay justice became "irrational" justice, by contrast to the activities of lawyers who were the "masters of a necessary and not widely understood science."[52] Similarly, abstract concepts of "public will" and "the voice of the people"[53] were privileged over local voices and local practices as the basis for policy and for law.

Local peacekeeping practices became particularly suspect in the early nineteenth century when popular uprisings in Boston, Philadelphia, and elsewhere taxed the capacity of local officials to keep order, and led to calls for reform.[54] The fee system that supported the activities of constables, sheriffs, watchmen, and justices of the peace was a particular focus of reformers. Arguing that the payment of lay magistrates by fee was a system in which "vice inheres,"[55] reformers attacked the fee system as the basis for the manipulation of justice for "personal" ends, and a reason for what they considered to be the vast numbers of "frivolous" cases before the courts.[56] These cases, said to be inspired by "'vindictiveness, malice or intemperance and thoughtlessness',"[57] produced, in turn, "corrupt, arbitrary, and lawless" procedures among justices of the peace.[58] Describing this justice as "rough," and the practices of lay magistrates as "haphazard"[59] and "obscure,"[60] reformers urged integration of the court system and the replacement of "mere village tribunal[s] for village peccadilloes"[61] with dignified settings conducive to distanced and "fair" decision-making. In this way (to use Max Weber's familiar description of a "depersonalized" bureaucracy), "love, hatred, and every personal, especially irrational and incalculable, feeling [could be excluded] from the execution of official tasks."[62]

Elimination of the fee system, while arguably a way of preventing abuse of justice by magistrates and police, was also a way of controlling the definition and organization of justice: how it should be administered, by whom, and for what kinds of problems. This, in turn, defined the terms in which access to justice was construed, and affected the power of ordinary people to define crime. In nineteenth century Philadelphia, for example, assaults and other nonproperty offenses that constituted the business of aldermen (urban justices of the peace) were described in the Philadelphia *Public Ledger* as "trifling . . . without benefit to anyone, and in most cases brought only to gratify a personal pique."[63] Yet battered wives, whose complaints constituted a significant proportion of aldermen's cases, used this access to law "as a tool in their struggle to define the power dynamic of the family."[64] At the same time, the power of lay magistrates, "child savers,"[65] constables and other "preprofessional" intervenors in cases such as these was constructed through the "fabricated" tales and "trivial" misdemeanors of those who appealed to them for judgment or assistance.[66]

The attack on decentralized procedures and decentralized compensation was of one piece with the trivialization of "neighborhood quarrels" as "petty" and of those who brought them as "thoughtless" people who *mis*used justice for "personal" ends. Reformers argued that there was "no need of a magistrate at every man's back door" and that "[n]eighborhood quarrels, petty depredations, [and] small-scale predatory activities . . . are best disposed of summarily," without "contentious procedure" but "within the limits of the law."[67]

The establishment of special tribunals for trivial cases created a hierarchy of judicial practice in which the irrational and trifling were assigned to "inferior" courts, or to the "community function" of such courts, [68] and designated as the territory of "administrative inspection and supervision and adjustment,"[69] while the prosecution, defense, and interrogation of serious matters were assigned to "superior" tribunals and "rigorously 'professional' experts."[70] This, in turn, institutionalized a hierarchy of class within the administration of justice that excluded or marginalized certain kinds of relationship, certain kinds of knowledge, and a certain kind of case.[71] These exclusions, produced in the context of nineteenth-century struggles, have shaped the legal representation of the "natural" world today, as evidenced in the assumption that first-instance criminal cases (in Massachusetts, cases typically heard by district court clerks and judges) are "*by their very nature* . . . amenable to pretrial disposition."[72] Such cases, "very serious to the participants or victims, and often most irritating in a crowded urban community,"[73] are implicitly and explicitly contrasted to property matters and property offenses, as the serious stuff of which public order is made and unmade.[74]

At the same time that marginal people with fabricated tales were excluded from elite legal arenas, however, Progressive reformers called for the reinsertion of lay magistrates outside the court but under its control. In this way, what reformers defined as the "casual arbitrariness" of lay practices was retained at the boundaries of the justice system, in a relationship of opposition to the "dignified" proceedings of the "rigorously professional" judge.[75]

In Massachusetts, the office of justice of the peace was gradually relegated "to the periphery of the court system" in a series of legislative changes beginning in 1858.[76] By 1902, a justice of the peace could no longer try civil or criminal cases unless designated a trial justice, or receive complaints and issue warrants unless appointed as a court clerk.[77] It is in this latter capacity, as Clerk Magistrate,[78] that the justice of the peace has been institutionalized in the Massachusetts court system. Assigned to "weed out" the irrational and mediate the petty, the clerk transforms "brainless" conflicts into everyday trouble or more serious crime, distinguishing neighborhood disturbances and lovers' quarrels from criminal matters requiring a more formal setting and the distanced decision-making of a judge.[79]

In the latest phase of what the legal profession describes as "court unification" in Massachusetts,[80] hearings before the court clerk are *required* before the issuance of "minor" criminal complaints as formal charges of crime.[81] These conflicts, characterized as "essential" rather than as legal matters because of their "social and interpersonal" nature, are relegated to what has been termed the "'community court' function" of the district court.[82] In this arena, where local values have priority over rights, the "interpersonal trouble" produced in family, class, and ethnic hierarchies can be monitored, while the (criminal) court is protected from "frivolous" matters. By distinguishing complaint hearings as marginal arenas within the legal system for controlling the problems of marginal people in society, the relevant public of the *court* proper (a professional audience of lawyers and administrators) is separated from the local audiences that the court is to serve.[83] At the same time, complaint hearings insinuate the law ever more pervasively into the everyday exchanges of neighborhood and family life.[84]

THE CONTRADICTIONS OF ORDINARY TROUBLE

The hierarchy embedded in the distinction between legal and community functions of the court is encoded in taxonomies (accepted by court staff and citizens alike) that classify events as "misdemeanors," "felonies," and so forth. These taxonomies objectify in "misrecognizable form" divisions of the social order that dictate what is serious and what is trivial in court as in social life more generally.[85] Hearings before a court clerk are practices that signal the ordinariness of the events involved, events that take place in the lives of people who are (in the words of the Clerk Magistrate in Greenfield) "overridingly the poor."

While show cause hearings confirm the substance of the ordinary, locating the interpersonal in the lives of the poor and the powerless, they also provide a time and a space at the courthouse for discovering the criminal *in* the everyday. The clerk's official role in the hearings is to determine whether there is "probable cause" that a crime has been committed, that is, whether "the elements of crime . . . appear among the facts elicited to support the charge."[86] He is urged to "refrain from initiating criminal proceedings where the conflict can be fairly resolved by something less"[87]; but he is instructed to issue a complaint where he has found probable cause if the complainant is unwilling to settle informally.

From this perspective, complaint hearings both confirm the ordinariness of poor people's problems and hint at their connection to hazard, danger, and crime. For example, in the complaint about the girdled tree, the clerk's interpretation of how a nuisance became "a principle thing" for the police and his suggestions for how "private" problems could be transformed into public ones if complainants expanded the relevant audience point to the porosity of the boundaries between crime and nuisance, and the relevance of social context to the definition of crime. In this complaint, the interpretive authority of the clerk is limited by the knowledge and power of the police, who filed the official complaint. In complaints initiated by citizens, the clerk has more leeway; but even so, his power to discover the criminal in the everyday is always constrained by the common sense that the problems brought by citizens are local matters.[88] Thus clerks experience the issuance of citizen complaints as problematic and as potentially subject to sanction (in the form of ridicule or reprimand), if their authority in this area is overused.[89]

The contradictions of a mandate permitting the clerk to discover crime in local disturbances, while urging him to keep these matters out of court, is a source of dynamic tension in complaint hearings. His power to manipulate the law by issuing criminal charges draws citizens to him with complaints; yet his skill in handling conflict informally secures his place as magistrate at the court. In a universe officially divided into private and public spheres, the clerk is positioned at the imaginary juncture of these domains, reproducing them by distinguishing "crime" from "garbage," but occasionally using garbage to reconfigure crime.[90] In this sense, the practice of gatekeeping becomes what Michel de Certeau has described as "a *way of using* imposed systems," "a practice of the order constructed by others [that] redistributes its space," creating "a certain play in that order, a space for maneuvers."[91] In effect, complaint hearings establish a zone of the "everyday" (the communal, the informal, the common sense) within the law, through which the law can be known in the clerk's practices of "naming" crime and "revealing" rights.[92] As a space where "*continuity . . .* give[s] place to *contiguity,*"[93] the hearings both limit law and extend its power through a clerk who "connects, by separation, classes and discourses."[94]

The clerk's capacity for maneuver depends, in part, on who the clerk is. In addition, there are differences among institutions. There are differences in the kind of legitimacy accorded to local matters at the courthouse, in the leeway given to the clerk in interpreting local violence as crime, and thus in the potential for unsettling established categories ("neighborhood disturbance," "lovers' quarrel," "kids pushing kids") through the exchanges of clerk and citizens.

In Greenfield, for example, the interpretation of show cause hearings as a site for local problems and of the court proper as the place of law is complicated by a historical tradition of resistance to the centralization of law and the consolidation of state power, and by a counterconvention of local governance and of commitment to a local way of life. This counterconvention is evident not only in struggles over control of the county court,[95] but in commitment to a locally controlled economy, politics, and culture as well.[96] At the courthouse, the contradictions of an ethos that affirms local distinctiveness and local control, on the one hand, and trivializes "local disturbances," on the other, produce the dynamic of complaint hearings where a "garbage" case encodes key issues of local identity and provides a vehicle for affirming this identity publicly through law.

Contemporary struggles over local identity in Greenfield are fought not only in hearings before the clerk, but in confrontations between labor and management, or between developers and citizens who want to limit the possibilities for transforming the face (and character) of the town. The next chapter examines some of these confrontations, considering how the responses of participants to one another provide an interpretive lens through which contemporary events in Greenfield and elsewhere are given meaning, reshaping local understandings of the past in this process.

CHAPTER 3

"THIS IS NOT CONEY ISLAND"

We take pleasure in recording the fact that never before was our beautiful town so well fitted to be the residing place and home of an educated, refined, industrious and common sense people as it is now. We have all the conveniences, and too many of the luxuries of the dwellers in the metropolis, with scarcely none of its miseries, its slums and scandals of official rascality to contend with, and we ought to be a happy and contented people.

From Selectmen's Annual Report
to the Town of Greenfield, 1895

In mid-1983, a strike by machinists against Greenfield's second largest employer, TRW-Greenfield Tap and Die Division (GTD), continued for weeks and dominated headlines in the town newspaper. At issue were proposed takebacks by management during upcoming contract negotiations.[1] The company defended its action as a response to a downturn in the national economy that had affected a number of local employers, some of whom had resorted to layoffs, others to temporary shutdowns. An editorial in the local paper, the *Greenfield Recorder*, condemned strikers for dividing workers from management and jeopardizing the stability of the town: "There are many workers at TRW-Greenfield Tap & Die Division who have given the best years of their productive lives to the factory, in some cases as many as 30 years. And in return, they've been given good wages, numerous benefits and a secure feeling that they would always have a job there. That relationship has been torn, set adrift by the 14-week-old strike that threatens the future of the workers, the plant itself, and the economic vitality of the entire community."[2] Strikers argued that adequate wages for local workers were of more benefit to the town than higher profits for company stockholders "such as National City Corp., Republic Steel and Standard Oil of Ohio who have no concern for us."[3]

The strike heightened local worry about the uncertain future of the small tool industry, a mainstay of Greenfield's economy since the late nineteenth century. Machinists were urged by some to "sit it out and wait,"[4] while others urged retraining programs. Debate on this issue was simply one manifestation of a pervasive tension about the town's identity and viability that appeared in other arenas as well. It was an implicit subtext in discussions about conversion of a vacant theater into a civic center, described by supporters as the "shining gem" in plans for downtown revitalization.[5] It was central in debates over a shift from representative town meeting (described as "obsolete" in a 1983 editorial in the *Greenfield Recorder*[6]) to centralized town management. Finally, concerns about the changing character of the town emerged in complaints to the criminal court over new neighbors and threatening life-styles. These debates, like others that had taken place in the eighteenth and nineteenth centuries, were carried out in imagery that evoked a particular vision of the town, as "quiet" but not "stagnant," as a place that could "grow and prosper"[7] while avoiding the "slums and miseries" that accompany development.[8]

The strike at Greenfield Tap and Die focused public attention on the fragility of the economic and social base on which this vision was constructed: an image of family firms, locally owned and financed, with local workers who share management's interests; an image of quiet, homogeneous neighborhoods where "[e]verybody gets along"[9]; and an image of a "pastoral" town in which "manufacturing operations are relatively hidden from view."[10] This ethic of a friendly community, where class is present but not the source of conflict, was challenged by the strike. One machinist declared in response to the rollbacks: "I don't give back anything. Not to a company that is making a profit."[11] The commissioner of the state Department of Commerce and Development told a meeting of the Franklin County Chamber of Commerce that corporate owners of GTD have "no ties with the community" and "will not hesitate closing [the company] . . . down."[12] (This was made clear with the closing of one of the company's two plants late in 1983, a decision that was described by the GTD general manager, apparently without irony, as "a commitment to Greenfield."[13])

Strikers were arrested, while salaried GTD employees were not, during an altercation that ensued between picketers and salaried employees in front of a GTD plant in June 1983. The negotiator for Local 274 of the United Electrical, Radio and Machine Workers of America said of the police action: "They slapped the union's hand but didn't slap the company's hand. They arrested union members but they didn't arrest the office worker who hit [the striker]."[14] The police response and reports in the news media suggested concern that the strike would alienate management and hasten the probability of a shutdown, posing an even greater threat to the local economy than the rollback.

The tap and die industry in Greenfield was the outgrowth of a bolt-cutting machine patented by John J. Grant, a machinist who moved to the town in 1869 or 1870 and subsequently became a partner of the Cooperative Machine Co.. (A tap drills interior threads for the bolt, while a die cuts exterior threads; they were heavily in demand by armament manufacturers during the Civil War, and immediately after the war were widely used in sewing machine production.) Grant's patent was purchased a year later by Solon L. Wiley, a native of Vermont, known as "something of a promoter who would follow money wherever it led," and by Charles P. Russell, a native of Greenfield. Together they established Wiley and Russell in 1872 to produce bolt-cutting machines on a large scale.[15]

By contrast to Wiley and Russell, Cooperative Machine was described by the *Greenfield Gazette & Courier* in the following words: "When industrious mechanics form a cooperative association for the purpose of placing the fruits of their skill and labor in the market without the aid of capitalist and employer, they do more for the cause of working men than all the 'Unions' and 'strikes' in the world, and will receive the hearty support of the public."[16]

While Wiley and Russell dominated the tap and die industry in the 1870s, other, smaller firms producing slightly different versions of the die opened during this period in Greenfield as well. By 1912, however, Wiley and Russell and Wells Brothers Company, the largest tap and die operations in Greenfield, merged under the name of Greenfield Tap and Die Corp. A third company was included 6 months later, and "over the next few years the network of interlocking and related businesses increased in complexity until much of Greenfield's well-being depended on the strength of that web."[17] By the 1980s when the strikes against GTD were in progress, the company had been owned and managed for decades by TRW, a multimillion dollar California-based defense contractor.

The contradictions of a company that symbolizes local enterprise, local ownership, and local control, but is at the same time portrayed as "a faceless management hundreds of miles removed from the scene of the action,"[18] are emblematic of the contradictions of the town itself. The survival of "community" in Greenfield has inevitably been dependent on people who are seen as lacking a commitment to the town: "captains of industry [who] are now accountants, lawyers, economists, advertising people and assorted hucksters."[19] The closing of one of the GTD plants in June 1983 and the proposed sale of another tap and die plant, owned by the Bendix Corporation, late that same year, provided ample support for this account of industrial indifference, and its local consequences.[20]

For many in the Greenfield business community, however, attracting outside investors is seen as vital to the town's survival. In the early 1980s, controversy over development focused on two vacant factory buildings and the efforts of town planners to encourage outside companies to invest in the buildings. One of the buildings was left vacant in the late 1970s when town voters refused to approve zoning changes that would have allowed expansion of the Millers Falls Company to a site on the other side of town. At the time of the strikes, a Boston-based developer was making plans for conversion of the building into a subsidized housing project, a plan opposed by local landlords. The required zoning change was rejected by a town-wide referendum in early 1982. Another vacant building, a factory warehouse, became the source of heated controversy in town when the Empire One Corporation, an investment firm based in Brattleboro, Vermont proposed establishing an indoor mall that would include wholesale and retail produce businesses, a delicatessen and restaurant, and a "family entertainment center with up to 100 video games."[21]

The proposed mall was described by the town planning director as a "proper and excellent use" of the abandoned building,[22] while opponents concentrated on the entertainment center, using language evocative of moral decline. This debate brought into focus the issues encoded in local controversies such as these, in which the conversion and transformation of former factory buildings by new developers became the terrain for debate about community demise. The chairwoman of the town selectmen told a crowded meeting at the Town Hall that she had "sincere reservations" that the town would support it. "This is not Hampton Beach. This is not Coney Island," she said.[23] Others described concerns about the new mall in terms of "noise, trash, odors from the fish market and congregations of young people."[24] While supporters portrayed the enterprise as inspired by a "family concept" that would sponsor "family activities," and spoke of working with churches and neighborhood residents to solve potential problems,[25] a Greenfield policeman remarked that "[t]he town doesn't have laws to back up what the police are expected to do" to maintain order in an "amusement center."[26]

The terms for this debate, couched in a rhetoric of moral turpitude and of righteous conduct, are familiar ones. The "specter" of a "games center,"[27] likened to the breakdown of orderly social life, is set up against a familiar vision of community stability. Family firms, quiet neighborhoods, and a refined and quiet way of life are contrasted with corporate greed, urban slums, and "Coney Island" or "Hampton Beach": the small, the local, and the familiar are set against strange practices and uncontrollable passions. "Family" and "community" are sacralized in these representations as "the last stronghold against The State, as the symbolic refuge from the intrusions of a public domain that constantly threatens ... [a] sense of privacy and self-determination."[28] Similar themes emerge in the self-portrayals of people in diverse localities in the contemporary United States and are repeated over time in histories that document recurrent contests over economy and identity.[29]

COMMERCE, "COMMON SENSE," AND COMMUNITY

In the early nineteenth century, Greenfield, a settlement of just over 1000 people, was the site of numerous textile mills and a cutlery works. As a small but thriving marketing and transportation center, it was developed through the collaboration of lawyers with successful local businessmen and wealthy investors from other parts of Massachusetts and from New York. German, Irish, and English immigrants worked in the mills, creating a stratified population of foreign-born laborers and skilled mechanics, on the one hand, and native-born lawyers, merchants, and factory owners, on the other.[30]

This picture of hierarchy is interwoven, here as elsewhere, with tales of "family" and "community." Thus the man who financed what was by 1860 the town's major industry (the Green River Works, a cutlery factory), and the single largest property owner in Greenfield, Henry Clapp, is represented in present-day accounts as a public-spirited citizen who built single-family and two-family homes for factory workers, "influenced by his vision of the town as a village whose rural atmosphere must be protected at all costs from the typical consequences of industrialization." Clapp constructed a Greenfield in which he became the principal property owner of housing and factories populated with skilled and unskilled metalworkers, while "pursu[ing] his picture of Greenfield as a homogeneous community of well-spaced, individual houses."[31]

The population of this "community" had doubled by 1860 with the construction of railroads linking Greenfield to Boston, to New Haven, and north to Troy, New York. Decisions about the routing of railroad lines, shaped by translocal market considerations, contributed to the incorporation of local banks (which, in turn, financed the railroads), and Greenfield lawyers and other developers were important local participants. Hostility to this activity was framed in a discourse that contrasted community interests and values to "schemes developed in secret by lawyer-promoters and sustained by public land grants and tax revenue."[32] Yet it was in the context of these "schemes"—indeed, in opposition to them—that the contours of community were sketched, even as its demise was envisioned. "Community" became a project of the bankers and developers whose rival activities shaped the development of Greenfield and of neighboring villages, such as Turners Falls, where today people described as "the other half of America" by Greenfield residents continue to struggle with these visions of community.[33]

The decision to route a railroad line through Greenfield to North Adams and Troy in 1850 was ancillary to Fitchburg industrialist Alvah Crocker's interest in the development potential of other sites along the Connecticut River, and particularly the falls above the Montague canal. Crocker, already president of the Vermont and Massachusetts Railroad, joined with Greenfield bankers and industrialists to incorporate the Troy and Greenfield Railroad in 1848. Together with Wendell Davis, one of the directors of the Troy and Greenfield, Crocker instigated the move of the Green River Works, Greenfield's major employer in the 1860s, to Turners Falls in 1870, an action that was viewed with alarm by other Greenfield businessmen. To finance the development of the relocated company, envisioned as central to the industrial development of the new town, Crocker and others sought to incorporate a new bank, named after the Fitchburg financier. This effort was opposed by other Greenfield businessmen who saw the relocation of the cutlery factory as a certain setback to Greenfield's economy and as a vehicle for shifting economic power away from Greenfield to a nearbye neighbor. Davis, who died a few years later, was described in an obituary in the Greenfield paper as the

> one man who led the whole tribe into the wilderness of Turners Falls, and succeeded in making the waters of the Connecticut gush into revolving turbines with a prospect of getting more money out of aqua-pura than Moses did when he hit the trail and then the rock.[34]

The use of Greenfield's principal industry for the development of a major venture next door evoked well-known cultural stereotypes of corporate corruption and private greed, with lawyers and bankers as central players. This portrayal of self-interested industrial growth is continually juxtaposed in the official history of the town with the "shop-wise spirit of adventure" of resourceful Yankees. Its heroes, characterized as "shrewd machinists," are always shadowed (and occasionally eclipsed) by "citified financial experts."[35] Out of this tension the town emerged as the "refined, industrious and common sense people" described in the 1895 editorial cited at the outset of this chapter.

Stories about these everyday heroes shape both the image of Greenfield's past and interpretations of its present struggles. Among them, and occupying a central place, is John Grant, the mechanic who developed the first die, an adjustable bolt-cutter for which he received a patent in 1871. This was the forerunner of the device through which the tap and die industry was established in Greenfield.[36] Grant's family emigrated from England to Holyoke in 1848, and he moved to Greenfield from Northampton 20 years later to work in a local machine shop. According to legend, "a travelling tool peddlar stopped in at the shop one day and mentioned how profitable it might be to design a machine for cutting threads on bolts. . . . Grant got to work [and] in October, 1871, applied for and received a patent for an improved bolt-cutting device."[37] Together with other machinists, Grant formed the Cooperative Machine Company in 1871 to market his bolt-cutter, but he was soon hired by Wiley and Russell, a competing, much larger venture, representing Greenfield's established industrial community.

Other well-known figures whose activites have contributed to the portrait of Greenfield as a community of hard-working and "common sense people" are the Wells brothers. Sons of a Shelburne cutler, Frank and Frederick Wells developed an improved bolt-cutting device while working for Wiley and Russell and then left the larger company to establish their own shop. By 1890, financed by the Greenfield Savings Bank and the Franklin County Bank, they had become the Wells Brothers Company, employing 70 machinists. Today, this company is portrayed as still having the "feeling of shared enterprise and constant experimentation."[38] The Wells brothers are depicted as exemplary of "the native wits [sic] of industrious, inventive mechanics responding to local needs, whose products enhance the prospect for local self-sufficiency."[39]

In spite of major changes in the town's economy, in which mergers effaced the local base of tool companies to create satellites of large multinational corporations, the image of a community controlled from within is a vital part of today's myth about Greenfield's past. This myth is perpetuated in tales about the activities and public-spirited commitment of paternalistic financiers such as Henry Clapp, or about the civic contributions of machinists such as John Grant or the Wells brothers, whose move from immigrant employee to shop manager and owner embodies the ideals of a town heavily dependent on a translocal economy but where autonomy and independence remain key values.

Greenfield shops were unionized in the 1930s and 1940s, with the formation of the Industrial Association of Small Tool Workers at GTD in 1934, and subsequently, after much controversy, when employees at GTD plant #2 joined the United Electrical, Radio, and Machine Workers (UE) as local #274 in 1941. This move was attributed by opponents to outside instigation, and was represented as undermining what management perceived as the "family feeling" that prevailed in local companies.[40] Known since the 1920s as a banking town, Greenfield is nonetheless "reluctan[t] to see itself polarized along class lines."[41] Tales of the "good close relationship" of workers and management and of transformations from immigrant worker to corporate manager suggest the low salience of class in a town where poverty is present but, like the manufacturing operations that sustain the town's economy, "hidden from view."

The 17-week strike of 1983, together with layoffs in some industries and the changing configuration of homelessness in the area, brought the contradictions of family and market together in the public arena, hinting at the connections between them and revealing conflicts within the town about the meaning of "common sense" and of commitment to "the community." The agreement that ended the strike, described as "a significant compromise" from the company's original proposal,[42] resolved the immediate conflict in what workers described as "the best settlement the union could get under the circumstances."[43] The strike that achieved that settlement, the fifth and longest in Greenfield's history, represented more than a means to agreement, however. Like the move of the Green River Works to Turners Falls in 1870, the strike served as an "event of articulation,"[44] a moment when "people have to take sides, in terms of deeply entrenched moral imperatives and constraints."[45] With unemployment increasingly a subject of local comment, the strike highlighted the connections of each side to groups and interests typically constructed as "outside" community, indeed as definitive of what Greenfield was *not*: materialistic, self-interested, hierarchical, driven not by embeddedness in local relational networks, but by class interests, a desire for profit, and power.

HIERARCHY AND COMMUNITY

In May 1983, a front-page article in the *Greenfield Recorder* described the plight of Mark and Sandra Rich of Greenfield, who "put their three sons to bed in the family car one March night and drove around until morning to keep the heater running."[46] No longer simply the problem of "older alcoholic males," homelessness and emergency shelter were described in the local media at this time as increasingly affecting "families with children."[47] Similarly, unemployment (or the threat of unemployment) was perceived to be affecting a broad spectrum of Greenfield's working class, as machine tool companies closed plants and laid off workers. Articles in the *Greenfield Recorder* focused on this dimension of the economic downturn, describing men such as Gary Tracy, a machinist at the Bendix Corporation, who had changed jobs seven times within 5 years due to plant cutbacks, and was laid off in 1981. "There was a lot of bumping going on, but for a while I had enough seniority to stay on," Tracy was quoted as saying. "Then I was laid off for the first time about a year after I'd bought my first home. I wondered how I was going to pay the mortgage—if I would find a new job—if I would be called back. There was a lot of stress. My wife did her best to put up with me." Pictured on the front page of the *Recorder* washing dishes in his kitchen, with his 3-year-old daughter Kathryn sitting on the counter nearby, Tracy noted that he was "luckier than most of his former co-workers, whose wives did not have jobs." Tracy was called back in September 1981, but was laid off again the following May.[48] In an interview, the manager of employee relations at Bendix saw the future as "very bleak" due to slumping auto and construction industries.[49]

Stories such as these, together with the portrayal of companies such as GTD or Bendix as controlled by corporate owners and disrupted by angry strikers, document what French sociologist Pierre Bourdieu describes as "the inevitable, and inevitably interested relations imposed by kinship, neighbourhood, or work"[50] in towns such as Greenfield. The ideologies that shape the portrayal of workers and management as connected by a "family feeling" obscure the contradictions woven into these relationships. Specifically, they conceal how relationships are tied to the contingency of a market economy where labor is bought and sold, and where the morality of contract, rather than of "family feelings," governs the connections of employee to employer.[51]

Greenfield in the 1980s was hardly less stratified than it had been in the past. According to the 1980 census, 20% of the employed population of the town consisted of unskilled laborers, while just over 20% occupied managerial or specialized professional positions. These included lawyers, bankers, physicians, and other health care specialists employed at the Franklin County Medical Center in Greenfield or at the Farren Memorial Hospital, a private institution in Turners Falls.

(Nineteen percent of the labor force in Greenfield is employed in the health services.[52]) Financial institutions, central to the funding of the tap and die shops, the railroads, and the development of Turners Falls in the nineteenth century, continued to play a key role in the life of the town. In 1982 there were three commercial banks, a trust company, three savings banks, and a cooperative bank in Greenfield, which is described by the Chamber of Commerce as the "financial center" of Franklin County. People employed in the financial, insurance, and real estate industries accounted for 7% of the labor force in the town. As the county seat, the town houses the court, and most court staff, the district attorney, and many of the lawyers who appear there on a regular basis reside in Greenfield, and contribute to the town's collective image as "educated, refined, industrious and common sense."[53]

The mean family income in Greenfield in 1980 was $20,260, but this figure obscures the wide gap between the most affluent and most indigent neighborhoods. In the poorest area of the town, mean income was $13,603, and included substantial numbers of people (18% of 177 families) with an income below the official "poverty level." Thirty-three percent of these families were earning less than $10,000 per year. In another low-income neighborhood, 41% (185 of 450) of the families were earning less than $10,000 annually, and 15% were living beneath the poverty level. By contrast, in Greenfield's wealthiest neighborhood, the mean family income was $23,161, and 3% (12 of 377) of the families earned over $75,000 per year.[54]

These figures signal differences in the social configuration of family and neighborhood life in Greenfield. In the poorest neighborhoods, households are likely to be headed by women, most of the housing is occupied by renters, and over half of the population is in multiple housing units, many in units of three or more. In wealthier neighborhoods, by contrast, most households consist of married couples with children, most own their own homes, and single-family housing predominates.[55] While census divisions are imprecise, the rough distinctions documented in census tables are acknowledged in conversations with residents from the poor neighborhoods. They describe their own streets as "slums" and say police refer to these areas as "down in the hole." Similarly, social workers call these same neighborhoods "target areas" for their work. By contrast, the "High Street area" is known for its elegant homes, and as a haven for professionals.

These distinctions in quality of life are part of the context within which the economic downturn of the early 1980s was experienced in Greenfield. At stake in local debate about the GTD strike, as in earlier contests about the Greenfield "way," was a struggle about the very nature of the taken-for-granted in this rural New England town: about morality, rights, and virtue, and about the boundary between self-interest and collective good. By implying that profit, class difference, and power could be found at the very heart of "community" in its "family firms," the debates about development of Turners Falls in the late nineteenth century and the strike at GTD in the 1980s set the ideology of community in question; at the same time, the debates themselves were taken as evidence of community demise.

Events such as these occasionally break through what Pierre Bourdieu refers to as the "veil of enchanted relationships" that sustain some forms of domination,[56] but in Greenfield today conventional scripts for "community" and "family" are continually reinscribed in other town arenas. The courthouse, for example, is an institution perhaps most evocative of order and moderation in Greenfield's "way of life." Here, the use of law is both encouraged and denounced, as "brainless" and uncontrolled people from "the other half of America" are viewed as manipulating law for self-interested ends, while peace-loving citizens may turn to the court as a way of keeping order when no other third party is available. Law, then, is at the same time the source of order and of its disruption, and court use becomes a mark both of the disintegration of community and of efforts to maintain a particular way of life.[57]

This combination in the law—of "brainlessness" with unrestrained "outsiders"[58] and of virtue with a controlled (and controlling) self—reconstitutes the very dichotomy the GTD strike set in question. At the courthouse, "brainlessness" and lack of restraint become signs of distinction marking the boundaries between Greenfield's "way of life" and that of others in towns such as Turners Falls. This distinction locates self-interest *outside* community, obscuring the very contingency on which Greenfield's way of life rests. Just as GTD was the terrain on which family and community were constituted in the news media and interrogated by the strikers, so are complaint hearings the locale for the construction of a virtuous citizen in court.

"PEOPLE WANT TO COME
TO THE COURTHOUSE . . ."

The Franklin County courthouse, an imposing red brick building with white columns, stands prominently at a major intersection just beyond the center of Greenfield. Contest over the location of the courthouse (and of the county seat) in the early nineteenth century was emblematic of political rivalries between Greenfield and Deerfield over economic and cultural prominence in the region. (The parent town of Greenfield, Deerfield is located about 4 miles to the south along the Deerfield River.) Greenfield was successful in its petition to the legislature to be designated "shire town," and the first courthouse was constructed there in 1813 on what is presently known as "Bank Row." It was the site of governance and religious functions, as well as judicial ones, during the first half of the nineteenth century, but occasionally featured prominently in efforts to subvert established hierarchies.[59] The present structure, located near the site of the original one, houses not only the court, but the County Registry of Deeds, the Extension Service, and the Offices of the County Commissioners, described today as "the executive body of the county . . . , elected by the people and . . . responsive to the trend of opinions and thinking in their own counties."[60]

With a jurisdiction that includes 18 villages and towns in the county (ranging in size from 200 to just over 18,000 people in Greenfield itself), the courthouse is perceived in Greenfield as a "symbol of county government"[61] and has been at the center of recent struggles over the future of Franklin and other counties in the face of what are locally represented as efforts at "state take-over."[62] In a February 18, 1983 article in the *Greenfield Recorder*, Hampshire County Commissioner Robert Garvey was quoted as "serv[ing] notice on all those out there who have attempted to take over the functions of the counties: We're ready to fight." The article added that "the fight has been going on—with counties usually taking a defensive posture—for decades against bills for the state to assume control of traditional county functions, impose restrictions or do away with counties entirely."[63] Noting that "[i]n Massachusetts, counties count most in places that count least," the *Greenfield Recorder* described the county as "a buffer between town hall [in smaller towns] and state pressures," but added that "the cry of those communities has traditionally gone unheard in the cavernous halls of the Statehouse."[64]

The tension between state government and local government came to a head in 1978 with passage by the Massachusetts legislature of the Court Reorganization Act. This Act took budgetary and administrative control over courts away from local counties and located it in the office of a Chief Justice of the District Court Division, making court staff employees of the state.[65] Describing the Act as "rape" by the Commonwealth, and as an attempt to "wipe out county government," County Commissioners sitting in Greenfield also attempted to lock state employees out of the courthouse in 1980.[66] While this move ended with a Supreme Judicial Court injunction forcing them to keep the building open, it underscored once more the key role of the court-house as a site of struggle over local autonomy and identity.

The courthouse not only symbolizes the presence of the state in a building that stands for regional autonomy, but also encodes the complex relations of Greenfield elites to the immigrant and working class populations whose labor sustained the town economy for over a century. Court staff are descendants of these immigrants. Yet in managing the continuing stream of neighbor and family problems brought before them, the staff affirm a liberal order of self-disciplined restraint that excludes today's urban and working class poor as "irrational," and as products of a way of life characterized by "fighting." Placed at an intersection that separates the town's elite residential neighborhoods from its business district to the south, the courthouse stands in striking contrast to the transitional neighborhoods and urban slums that spread out to the east and west of the building, around the former sites of two of the town's major industries. The structure seems to stand guard. In colonial America, "holy watching"[67] was considered the responsibility of all members of a congregation. Today, the court's responsibility to "keep watch" stems from the "retreat" of schools, churches, families—"even the individual" (to paraphrase a comment by the Clerk Magistrate).

Court staff share concerns expressed by others and articulated on a daily basis in the local paper regarding the changing face of the town: loitering youth, runaway teenage girls, and more serious juvenile crime; neighborhoods where "there is nothing that pulls people together," and transients roam the streets; and the vacant buildings left as companies that were the town's major employers and symbolize its place in history, move to other regions. Debate over these problems, focused at times on proposals for new businesses (like the mall and amusement center) or on discussion of existing ones (the "Final Frontier Arcade," popular with young people, but said to encourage loiterers),[68] is regularly reenacted at the courthouse in charges of delinquency and crime. The use of official language for describing these problems distances them from what one court clerk described as "neighborhood standards," likening them instead to behavior that "possibly would not be tolerated even in Springfield or New York." At the same time, these conflicts are perceived as signs that "the way they live in the ghettos" is rapidly moving in on Greenfield's "way."

The Court Reorganization Act of 1978 channelled these matters to show cause hearings before the court clerk, who was given charge of the "community function" of the court.[69] While this division of functions affected how the court's caseload was managed, the local meanings of going to court blur official distinctions between "legal" and "community" functions. For court officials in Franklin County, the "community function" of the court means that an institution controlled to an increasing degree by the Commonwealth can also be used to shape "the good moral order of the county."[70] It is in this sense that one of the clerks described his role as "like a watchdog," distinguishing himself from the police, who "have to handle [a conflict] right then." The concept of clerk as watchdog softens the boundary between "gatekeeping" for the court and "watching" in the community, tying the contemporary order of law to a colonial order in which local peacekeeping involved lay magistrates who depended on citizen complainants for the judicial governance of county life.

The symbolism of the courthouse as a locus of moral order extends beyond court staff to those who appear there voluntarily or involuntarily as complainants and defendants. The meaning of "moral sense" is contested in these appearances, and the order that the courthouse represents is constituted, in part, through diverse struggles over local politics, local identities, and the meaning of crime that take place there. For the parties to complaints, the "community function" of the court *is* the law, and the language and practice of complaining are legal forms, turning the court into a neighborhood battleground, as participants use this law as a resource in local power struggles. The clerks tend to see these struggles as feuds, and matters that will "never be solved" unless one of the parties moves away. But their very enactment at the courthouse provides a kind of morality play, a "social drama" through which judges, attorneys, clerks, and other court staff construct themselves as people of restraint and moderation.[71] Like the strikers in confrontations at Greenfield Tap and Die, whose legal demands were portrayed as "tearing" their relationship with a paternalistic management and threatening the economic stability of the town, so too are unruly "garbage people" at the courthouse depicted as requiring the discipline of a paternalistic clerk, and as threatening the order represented by the courthouse because of their entitlement as *subjects* of law.

What are official strategies for keeping trouble "out of court" and how do they vary from clerk to clerk? Through an analysis of complaint hearings in Greenfield and in Salem, Massachusetts, the next chapter compares two courts to illustrate differences in the capacity of clerks to govern those before them, and to suggest that the greater "space for maneuver" of clerks in Greenfield is shaped by the meaning of the courthouse and of law in an area with an active tradition of resistance to centralized authority. By focusing on the different governing capacities of clerks at each court, I want to explore how translocal processes that marginalize lay procedures and privilege a professional culture of law are remade according to local patterns and particular histories.

CHAPTER 4

RIGHTS AND THE INTERPRETATION OF CRIME

The discovery of injustice . . . depends upon the feeling that one has rights.

Pierre Bourdieu,
The Force of Law, 1987

The local vernacular of "rights" is transformed into official charges of crime or everyday trouble in the exchanges of court staff with citizen complainants. This transformation is accomplished through the "governing" capacity of the court clerk. This capacity is a form of power, a relationship, according to Michel Foucault, that is "a way of acting upon an acting subject or acting subjects by virtue of their acting or being capable of action." The exercise of power by the clerk "incites, . . . induces, . . . seduces, . . . makes easier or more difficult" the actions of those before him.[1]

In a related discussion, Anthony Giddens describes power as "transformative capacity," that is, it is *"harnessed to actors' attempts to get others to comply with their wants.* Power, in this relational sense, concerns the capability of actors to secure outcomes where the realisation of these outcomes depends upon the agency of others."[2]

This chapter analyzes "governance" in the sense suggested by Foucault and Giddens. This requires a reframing of the way "control" is understood in the analysis of power. Control will be located *in* the relationship of clerk to citizens. That is, control is situated in the clerk's practical mastery of local ways and local knowledge (both at the court and in surrounding towns) and in his capacity to translate this skill into a definition of events that "cools out" complainants, by recognizing the legitimacy of their complaint. In this way the clerk secures their complicity in a decision that typically limits their access to the court while expanding his own options in monitoring the course of their trouble.[3]

Central to this analysis of the clerk's power is the recognition that practical mastery also *constrains* the clerk, however, as Pierre Bourdieu's discussion of this concept implies.[4] Constraint follows from engagement in a field of action, "a total structure of actions brought to bear upon possible actions,"[5] and on the key place of time in this engagement. Practice "unfolds in time."[6] This means not only that the exchanges of a clerk with specific citizens may have both a history and a future that shapes their interaction, but that the social positioning of the clerk in *any* case implies an ongoing relation of dependence with citizens whose complaints are the source of his authority at the court.

Drawing on policy statements regarding the complaint procedure, and on material from fieldwork in two Massachusetts district courts (the Franklin County District Court in Greenfield and the District Court of Essex in Salem), I suggest ways in which the social and institutional context of complaining shapes the capacity of clerks in each court to govern those who appear before them with complaints.

THE LEGAL CONSTRUCTION
OF THE CLERK AS NONLEGAL

The special place in law of the complaint, or show cause hearing is indicated by the discourse of invisibility, of practicality, and of common sense that dominates official descriptions of the procedure. In the *Standards of Judicial Practice*, an administrative regulation circulated by the Chief Justice of the District Court Division to the district courts of the Commonwealth, complaint hearings are distinguished from criminal proceedings not only by their privacy, but by their quality as "one of the least visible" of district court proceedings.[7] Privacy is explained on grounds of protecting the rights of the accused from frivolous complaints, and the presumption that complaints are likely to be frivolous is implied in the absence of provision for a right to counsel. When present, counsel is formally subordinate to the clerk.[8] Thus procedural safeguards depend on "the self-accountability of the magistrate himself."[9]

Because the complaint process technically precedes the criminal process, clerks are not required to have legal training. Rather, decisions in complaint hearings are to be based on "practical considerations of everyday life on which reasonable and prudent men [sic], not legal technicians, act." In particular, clerks "must avoid turning these hearings into informal trials."[10] Informal rather than formal, lay rather than professional, and common sense rather than legal, the hearings are officially distinguished as the province of local institutions, local men, and local knowledge.[11]

The emphasis on practical knowledge and on standards of "reasonableness" rather than on legal rules in official descriptions of the clerk's role are reminiscent of discussions about the place of "practical skill" in policing.[12] Like the police patrolman, clerks are at the same time both "law officers" and "peace officers,"[13] and the two practices imply quite a different, and to some extent contradictory, stance. Thus while the position of "law officer" implies distance and externality, an effective "peace officer" must "know the people" and this means possessing "an immensely detailed factual knowledge of his beat." On skid-row, for example, officers "seek to install themselves in the center of people's lives and let the consciousness of their presence play the part of conscience."[14]

Just as knowing the people and knowing the situation are seen as crucial to the practical skill of police work, so are common sense and practical knowledge seen as central to the clerk's skill in handling the "everyday" problems of people who come to him with complaints. Official manuals of judicial practice distinguish this situational knowledge from the technical skill involved in the practice of law. Like police, clerks are often brought into the "then and there" of emergent problems, and must determine, in terms of common sense reasoning and "the attitudes of persons involved," whether "some development has reached a critical stage, ripe for [offical] . . . interest."[15]

FRAMING LOCAL TROUBLE AS CRIME

Conflicts brought before the clerk range from the most mundane to the most serious. Stories about burned pies, torn clothes, and broken "big wheels" toys compete for the clerk's attention with accounts of beating, sexual abuse, and attacks with knives or "numchuks," and tell of hostile encounters between neighbors, lovers, or friends, between parent and child, or between husband and wife. Landlords complain about tenants who refuse to move, while tenants complain about "wrongful acts" of a lessor. Employers charge employees with trespassing once their jobs have been terminated, citizens complain about eccentric outpatients from local mental institutions, and town residents appear at the courthouse in protest against the actions of corporations, such as the spraying of herbicides along power lines by the Western Massachusetts Electric Company.

Paradoxically, while court policy underscores the noncriminal nature of complaint hearings, complainants must transform narratives of trouble such as these into a discourse of crime and of legal entitlement in order to be granted a hearing. Thus complaint applications describe assault and battery, threats, or disturbing the peace; defacing or damaging public property, trespassing, and health code violations; and claims of harassment, of "staring," and of other "aggravations" for which complainants feel entitled to the protection of law.[16]

Converting tales of acrimony and injustice into the official language of the Massachusetts General Laws involves the clerk and the complainant in a complex exchange that is dominated by the clerk, although local voices and experiences occasionally emerge with force and clarity.[17] Consider, for example, the following description of trouble by a young working class man from the town of Salem in a complaint application he filed with the clerk at the District Court of Essex in eastern Massachusetts:

> They hit my wife with Baseball Bat
>   and it was Dismissed.
> We tryied mediation. it failed
> They always yell at us
> They park their car in our way
> they stair at my wife
> they walk real close to her
> they stair in our windows
> they make verbel threats to run us out of neighborhood.
> Plus anything and everything to agravate

In another application submitted to the same court, a retired blue-collar worker in his early fifties described his encounter with a neighbor as he walked his dogs near the neighbor's house early one morning. According to his statement, the neighbor "complained of the presence of me and my dogs, and insisted that I get off the property." The description continued:

> I replied that we were on a public way, and therefore had no reason to leave, whereupon he committed the tort of battery by his forceful grasp of my jacket, and after threatening me with his intent to personally "rub any shit on his lawn into my face," he then forcefully shoved me backward, which caused my uncontrolled fall upon one of my dogs.
>
> It is my contention that his act of assault and battery was an interference of my rights to (1) freedom from bodily

injury to myself and my dog, (2) freedom from threats of any kind, and (3) freedom from the mental stress or suffering related to, not only the anxiety of the given incident and threat, but also the concern for the physical condition of myself (I retired early to avoid stress) and my dog, who now has a physical problem.

At the Essex court, complainants must fill in their own application forms, with only occasional, and hurried, assistance from an overworked typist in the clerk's office. The heavy criminal caseload at this court[18] means that clerical assistants have little time to devote to citizen complainants. The office where applications are submitted is typically filled with court officials, attorneys, police, and parties to incidents of crime. The atmosphere is confused. Busy, often harried officials preside over an office where private complainants may sit or stand for up to an hour waiting for assistance or for a hearing. When applicants for a complaint make themselves known, they are simply given the complaint application form; if they ask for assistance, this typically involves confirmation that the words used by the complainant to describe an event are acceptable. At times, a clerical assistant may provide a colloquial term or phrase that is part of a local vocabulary of trouble shared by staff in the clerk's office and those who come with complaints.

"Harassment," for example, a term used repeatedly on complaint forms at the Essex court, was often supplied by office staff when they were asked for an appropriate word to describe the recurring calls, visits, or threatening statements of a lover, husband, or other intimate. This appears on complaint forms as "violent harassment," "constant harassment and threats," or as "harassment . . . [so that] I have been afraid for my life." Other terms that appear repeatedly on complaint forms include "threats" ("threatening gestures," "threatening phone calls," threatening words) and "violence" ("violent temper," "violent actions," "violent harassment," "violent" streets). "Assault," the most frequent charge on citizen complaint applications, describes actions as various as "hitting," "poking," "punching," "kicking," "shoving," "dragging" along a sidewalk, throwing through a screen door, and chasing with a butterknife. Terms such as these provide a colorful, but relatively formulaic popular discourse of crime, and encode a broad range of social interactions and political contests.

At the Franklin County court in Greenfield, Massachusetts, complaint applications are more formal documents than in Essex, and it is the clerks, rather than complainants, who provide an official description of crime. Clerks in Essex County rarely give assistance in the application process and other staff are occupied with more important court business. In Franklin County, by contrast, the clerks tend to be involved in framing a complaint from the first appearance of complainants at the courthouse. The caseload is far smaller in Franklin County,[19] and the interaction of clerk with parties to complaints is more intimate, although the documents produced by this interaction are more legally standardized than in Essex.

In over-the-counter conversations, the Franklin County clerk works with complainant accounts to determine the appropriate charge, referring specifically in the application to crimes described in the General Laws, with citations to the appropriate chapter and section of the criminal code. For example, in a complaint brought by a 30-year-old woman from Turners Falls about a street fight involving her 11-old-daughter and another girl, the conflict was defined as "266-127, Willful Destruction of Property," and the complaint application provided information about the value of the property ($20), the name of the owner, the date of the incident, and the place where it occurred. The only written description of the conflict appeared in a small space provided for information about "property taken": "cut Marya's blue jean skirt in 1/2 with a jack-knife after officer told Teri to return it to her, laughed and walked away. Threatened to beat Marya up on her way to or from school, said they would kill her."

In another case, also from Franklin County, an elderly woman came to the courthouse complaining that her 20-year-old grandson was keeping her up all night while he played loud music or partied with his friends. She was asked by the clerk whether the grandson had destroyed any property or done anything to threaten their safety. When she replied that he burned candles in his room, the clerk suggested that the grandson's behavior constituted a threat, since their house could burn down if the candles were left unattended. He filed an application for "threat to commit a crime" on her behalf, citing Chapter 275, Section 2 of the Massachusetts criminal code.

A third complaint application in Franklin County, filed by a 17-year-old woman against her foster parents, joined her voice with that of the clerk to describe fights in the parents' yard and in a laundromat in which "Susan's hair was pulled, shoved around and draged [sic] on the tar, knocked down on the tar. My neck was squeezed. I was kicked out—my clothes were thrown outside—my pocket-book was scattered in the brush behind the house where RD [her foster father] threw it." The complaint application defined this encounter as "AandB" and cited Chapter 265, Section 13A of the criminal code.

Some complainants in Franklin County are more accustomed to using the official language of crime, and frame incidents themselves in more technical terms. A young man who came to the courthouse to complain that his ex-girl-friend's father had threatened to kill him if he appeared again at their house, described the incident as "threat to commit a crime, to wit murder." This framing of the incident was accepted as appropriate terminology at filing, although it was subsequently contested during the hearing by the clerk, who explained that "threat to commit a crime *is* a crime and it *isn't* a crime." In this case, he argued it was not a crime, because "intent" was lacking. For intent to be present "he would have had to take positive action, like chasing you out of his yard with a hammer or something."

In both courts, descriptions of trouble on complaint forms set the frame for hearings in which official accounts of crime are matched by the clerk with complainants' tales of aggravation, harassment, or of violations of their rights to "freedoms" of various kinds. This juxtaposition of official crime to normal trouble becomes the basis of the clerk's decision to continue or to deny a complaint, or of a complainant's decision to withdraw.

LEGAL TALK AND MORAL TALK: THE POWER OF "COMMON SENSE"

In Franklin County, the more technical description of an incident on the complaint form is the starting point of a hearing in which the complainant is permitted to "tell his own story." The telling is monitored by the clerk, however, in ways that limit the scope of the story and structure the sequence in which it is told. In Essex, the clerk reads (or may ask the complainant to read) the more colloquial account provided by complainants on the application form, and uses this as a basis for his own characterization of "real" crime. In both courts, a key feature of the complaint procedure is the definition of the same events alternately as "legal" and as "everyday," and the regular juxtaposition of legal talk and more distanced decision-making, with common sense rhetoric and more intimate conversational styles in the construction of incidents of trouble. In a procedure that embeds "the formal in the informal and the informal in the formal,"[20] show cause hearings connect the official power of state law to the more subtle power of conversations and counselling. This creates what Pierre Bourdieu terms the "double reality" of domination, which is both visible (as the imposition of a decision to dismiss by the clerk), and invisible (as the "choice" to withdraw by a complainant). Bourdieu describes this form of domination as violence which is both "undergone" and "chosen."[21]

The definition and redefinition of complaints are carried out in a setting that is intermittently structured and chaotic, solemn and carnivalesque, usually dominated by the questioning of a clerk acting as both attorney and judge, but sometimes dissolving into an undisciplined shouting match in which judge becomes bystander. These features are characteristic of hearings that are no more than cursory exchanges in a crowded office, as well as of proceedings conducted in a more formal setting, surrounded by the symbolism of law.[22]

At the Franklin County court, show cause hearings are held in the juvenile courtroom, a setting that is smaller and more intimate than the regular courtroom, but that evokes the formal atmosphere of a criminal trial. The clerk sits at a raised bench with the parties facing him at a table below, and opens each hearing with the following statement:

> For the record, this is a "show cause" hearing scheduled on behalf of _____, on a complaint application by _____, alleging _____. This is not a trial; it is not a mini-trial. You will not be found guilty or not guilty. I do not have to have evidence beyond a reasonable doubt: Just evidence enough to make a reasonable person believe that you *could* have done it. You do have a right to have an attorney. I cannot, at this stage appoint an attorney for you, but you may obtain one at your own expense. Would you like time to obtain counsel? . . . Do you have any questions? First I'll hear from [the complainant], and then you [the defendant] will have a chance to tell your story.

This introduction establishes the official quality of the hearing, while underscoring the fact that it is *not* a formal legal event. Proceedings are recorded, and the clerk directs questions to each of the parties in turn, dictating who will speak and in what order, and eliciting the amount and type of information he wants. While the complainant and respondent are each allowed to present their versions of an incident, the clerk may limit what they say, directing each party to "restrict yourself to the date and time of this complaint." The style of the hearings typifies that described by J. Maxwell Atkinson and Paul Drew for courtroom examination, in which there is a fixed "turn order" and turns are organized into question-and-answer pairs.[23] For example, in a hearing on a complaint of assault and disturbing the peace brought by an older man against his neighbor, the owner of a motorcycle business, the following exchange took place between clerk and complainant:

Clerk [to complainant]: Where do you reside? Where's your property in relation to his?
Complainant: It's right next door.
Clerk: Is that your home?
Complainant: Yes.
Clerk: What happened?
Complainant: It started on Saturday.
Clerk: What time of day?
Complainant: In the afternoon. . . . I just kept hearing that awful noise of motorcycles. He's going around and around the track and it just got on my nerves. . . . I walked over and I said, "Andy, I'd like to talk to you." And he poked me in the chest. So I called the police. I asked the police about it, and they told me to fill out a complaint for assault and battery.
Clerk: What time of day do they ride out there?
Complainant: All day long.

Control of the exchange of talk in a hearing allows the clerk to move from formality to what one clerk in Franklin County termed "little chats," stopping the tape recorder to go "off the record," or transforming an interrogation into what this same clerk described as a "little sermon." Speaking to teenagers who were in court on cross-complaints of assault, for example, he counselled:

Forget about these gangs. You don't have to be a macho man, because that's what gets you in trouble. . . . Don't try to impress people. . . . When you grow up, all these kids who are so important right now, you won't see any of them again. This is really only a little part of your life. But you don't want to screw yourself up now. Sometime, you're going to want to do something, but you'll have a criminal record. You've got to think about the consequences.

These moments off the record create spaces for more intimate conversation in which metaphors of responsibility, of restraint, of neighborliness, or of good parenting become the basis for persuasion that parties should "choose" to "get along." In this context, assertion of rights or charges of crime by a complainant are made problematic, the demands of a greedy or unsocialized self unattuned to collective needs in which each person must "show a little concern."

In another case, involving adults and children from Turners Falls who were in repeated fights over the presence of unwanted neighbors, the clerk went "off the record" to admonish the participants that they should "begin acting like adults and not like children." Asking, "What are you folks going to do about this problem with the children?" and explaining that if the case went to court "none of the peripheral issues—about noise, disturbances, disagreements—are going to be admitted into evidence," the clerk attempted to resolve the problem with a lecture that placed responsibility for the fighting—and for its control—with the parents, reframing what had been defined at filing as "assault," into an everyday problem of parental control and self-discipline. These procedural strategies create a space for ordinary talk in the context of a courtroom interrogation directed by the clerk, and allow the clerk to move between morality and law, keeping mostly to what one clerk termed "the middle area between" them, but moving "as far as possible to one side or the other" to accomplish specific ends.

In Salem, the complaint hearings for the Essex County court are held in a small, cluttered office assigned to the most junior clerk at the court. The filing system for citizen complaints at this court is poor; proceedings are frequently interrupted by phone calls, by secretaries needing papers on the clerk's desk, or by the clerk's efforts to locate information in an adjoining room. The problems of conducting the hearings with decorum are further complicated by the brief time alotted to the hearings each week (from 11 A.M. to 12 noon on certain weekdays), and the 15-minute period provided for each case. Hearings on citizen complaints are uneasily positioned between traffic hearings (which normally spill over into the time set aside for citizen complaints) and lunch, so that complaint hearings are often crowded into the last hour of a busy morning.

While the formality of a courtroom with clerk as judge is lacking in Essex hearings, the interpenetration of legal talk with everyday talk resembles that in Franklin County, in proceedings that are partly structured as a series of directive questions from the clerk, and partly constructed as counselling sessions with clerk as therapist. For example, in an assault and battery complaint brought to the Essex court by a middle class woman against her former husband, the clerk moved from questions about the incident to advice about the relationship. He rejected the complainant's contention that her ex-husband's actions in "grabbing" and "pushing" her in a restaurant during a dispute over visitation rights constituted assault, saying that he would "let this thing go today"; but after the defendant's departure, he turned to the woman and said:

> "If you are turning those kids against their father, you shouldn't be doing it." [And he added:] "Because he's still their father, even if he does have some emotional problems.

> . . . When a person upsets you, you've got to ask why. Is
> it me? You've got to get your own act together first! . . .
> You've got to teach those kids to love their father!"

Like the clerks in Franklin County, this clerk structured hearings into
segments in which morality was juxtaposed to law, turning to lectures
about responsibility and maturity after dismissing claims of entitlement
or charges of crime as inappropriate.

In another complaint, which the Essex clerk described as a "lover's
quarrel," a young woman brought a charge of harassment against her
former boyfriend for calling her late at night. The boyfriend, who
explained that he had called because he wanted the engagement ring
he gave her returned, said that the calls would stop. The complainant
insisted that she was afraid he would hurt her, and asked the clerk, in
tears, if "There's no way I can have a restraining order put on him"?
The clerk responded that this was not possible because entitlement to
a restraining order required that "he has to live in the house with
you," and added, "there's no such crime as harassment. I should be
dismissing this. If he threatens you, that's different." He turned to the
boyfriend, however, and said: "You're a full grown man. You don't
want someone who doesn't love you. You get married, have children,
end up in probate court. And you have a serious criminal charge. You
might end up in state prison. I'm going to continue this. But *I want
you to stay away from her.*"

Sermons such as these, and the dismissals to which they are frequently linked, reframe complainants' experiences of a "right" to
protection by the court into the terms of familiar relational hierarchies,
constituting morality in ways that reproduce the dynamics of power
from which complaints emerge in the first place.[24] In another complaint of harassment brought to the Essex clerk, a young woman
described the "violent actions" of her former boyfriend, and her fear
"that he will kill or hurt me in some way when I'm not expecting it."
The defendant did not appear for the hearing, but the clerk dismissed
her complaint, again on grounds that there is "no such crime" as
harassment. He counselled her, however, that "if he bothers you again,
file the right complaint and we'll issue it quick"; and he suggested that
she might bring a complaint of trespassing, if the defendant was on her
property. Appalled, the woman exclaimed, "You mean, because I used
the wrong word? . . . He didn't show up, and nothing happens?" And
she added, "Next time he sees me he's going to laugh. I just wanted
to let him know that if he bothers me any more he'll be in trouble. I
couldn't tell him that, his father couldn't tell him that—so I hoped the
courthouse people could!"

In this Essex case, the complainant's application was dismissed and her boyfriend successfully challenged the authority of the court by ignoring, without penalty, a summons. In this way the hearing reproduced the gender inequality within which the conflict was structured, intensifying, rather than diminishing, the complainant's sense of disempowerment. In hearings such as these, legal entitlement is constituted as the privilege of people who are aready advantaged by hierarchies that are inextricable from the "common sense" that men harass women, and that it is the responsibility of women to "get their act together" and avoid alienating their children from the men who abuse them.

THE PARADOX OF CONTROL AND CONSTRAINT

In spite of the ways in which clerks at each court control the complaint procedure, some hearings are dominated by the intensity of specific conflicts, as these are shaped by experienced parties or through collective actions that challenge the order of the court. This level of conflict is not simply a matter of strategic action by practiced complainants (although this also occurs) but is a consequence of what Rick Fantasia has termed "the collective chemistry of intragroup relations" in which "something new is created in the context of conflict."[25] In some hearings, alternate forms of "sense" emerge from the complaint process, even as they disrupt it. Complainants may discover "rights" or create, in an episodic and tentative way, forms of action and relationship that challenge conventional practice. Such hearings reveal some of the ways that accountability is located *in* practice, "embodied within the stream of conduct" of agents, rather than in self-consciously "intentional" strategies.[26]

The potential for invention of rights in complaint hearings is located in the relationship of clerk to complainants, as this is structured by trial court policy, as well as by local trial court practice. Invention, or creativity, is a dimension of the clerk's capacity for governance, or in Foucault's words, his capacity "to structure the possible field of action of others."[27] At the Essex court, the clerk's capacity for governance is constrained by his position at a court where the complaint process is marginalized. Paradoxically, as I argue in more detail in Chapter 5, this also limits the possibilities for invention by those who appear before him with complaints. In Franklin County, by contrast, where the tradition of district courts as "peoples' courts" is strong, the complaint procedure is a more central function of the court. This not only empowers the clerk in controlling the troubles of those who appear

before him, but it also empowers citizens, on whom the clerk is dependent if he is to accomplish his work at the court.[28]

The interdependence of clerk and citizens in Franklin County is
most apparent in a style of complaint management that emphasizes
persuasion over coercion; but it is also reflected in the capacity of parties collectively to transform trouble into crime, in spite of the clerk's
judgment that a particular complaint does not belong in court. The
following case provides an example. In this hearing, control of the outcome by complainants was affected by the intimate ties linking the
three parties to one another, on the one hand, and the shallow relationship of the parties to the clerk, on the other.

The complaint was brought by Nina Brown, a mild-mannered, 30-
year-old woman, against Karen Call, a person Nina described as "a
paying customer" at the Dairy Mart store where she worked. Robert
Kelly, whose relationship to the two women only became clear well
into the hearing, was also present. Nina said in the complaint this
involved "an assault with a pumpkin." The meaning of this case gradually unfolded in a complicated story of passion and vengeance in
which a brother and sister were protagonists. Unlike most Franklin
County hearings, where the clerk directs the sequence of events and
shapes the outcome, in this one he gradually became more spectator
than participant, allowing Robert (who had no official standing in the
complaint) to determine both how the complaint should be defined
and the outcome of the hearing.[29]

Asked by the clerk to begin with an account of the incident,
Nina said:

> Nina: Well, she [Karen] came into Dairy Mart—she was a
> paying customer—I know her from years back in Vermont.
> She went out the door and I went out after her. It was 11
> and I was going to close up. I went through the rocks, I got
> out by the pumps and I saw a pumpkin on the side of her
> truck. I said to her, "Look, there's a pumpkin," and she
> picked it up and threw it at me.
> Clerk: That's all that happened? Nothing happened before
> at the store?
> Nina: No.
> Clerk [to Karen]: You want to say something?
> Karen: I did go into the store and I was a paying customer.
> She did say there was a pumpkin, I picked it up and threw it.
> It was just a little pumpkin. It fell on the ground and broke.
> Clerk: Pumpkins have a way of doin' that when they hit
> the ground.

> Nina: I didn't hear her say it. I did see her throw it.
> Karen: The pumpkin never hit her sir, it hit the ground and splashed.

The clerk's attempt to defuse the tension in the room with his wry comment about pumpkins was unsuccessful. Each answer to his questions led further into a tale of violence that went back over a decade, and involved Nina, Karen, and Karen's half-brother Robert in what was later revealed as a lover's triangle. Karen and Robert were engaged in an ongoing struggle, with Nina as trophy. The incident with the pumpkin was one in a series of retaliatory actions in which Karen was attempting to reclaim Nina as her lover from her brother. As the plot became increasingly complex, the clerk allowed Robert to describe efforts by his sister to burn down the house he lived in with Nina, assaults by Robert on Karen's present lover, and other violent exchanges over a period of years as the parties moved from Vermont to Massachusetts and recreated their battle in different courtroom arenas.

Much of the hearing was taken over by heated exchanges between Karen and Robert, while Nina listened passively. Finally, the clerk, who pointed out that "the pumpkin is just a sideline here," suggested that "You evidently have a problem, but it seems the problem should be in Vermont, not in Greenfield." Robert insisted however that "there was an assault and battery. . . . Anything you pick up is an assault" and added in a threatening tone: "You sayin' you aren't goin' to do anything about this?" The clerk responded:

> Clerk: I didn't say that, but the family part is in Vermont.
> Karen: The real problem is between me and her. I'll give her restitution for her clothes.
> Robert: I want this continued. . . . I want it to go to court.
> Clerk [looking at Nina, who nods]: I can do that, but this isn't going to solve the problem. It's just the tip of the iceberg. [And again addressing Nina]: You want it? She threw the pumpkin?
> Nina: Yes.
> Clerk: Alright.

In this complaint, Karen and Robert transformed a hearing about assault into a reenactment of family history, "governing" the clerk with a narrative of violence in which he became complicitous by permitting them to use "a sideline" to justify issuance of a criminal charge. The parties in this case, experienced through many years of involvement with the court system, "knew" the law, but the clerk did not "know" the parties, in the sense that the violent subtexts of intimacy that dominated the hearing were unfathomable to him. "I must lead an awful simple life," the clerk once commented after another hearing about ongoing hostility. Unlike other complaints of family or neighborhood battles, however, which he termed "brainless," in the pumpkin case he remarked, "That's a situation where somebody's goin' to end up dead. That guy doesn't seem to be too smart. He woke up to girls one day and it happened to be his sister's girlfriend. This charge [the pumpkin assault] doesn't mean anything."

Other hearings at the Franklin County court, in which the complaint procedure became an instrument of political action in neighborhood racial confrontations, were also "taken over" through the collective action of parties.[30] These actions displaced the routine of questions and answers interspersed with little chats, transforming the clerk into an umpire who called "Time!" as he sought to define as "legal" space what had been lived by participants as a neighborhood battleground. "We don't get into any backyard arguments here," the clerk would note in these situations, pointing out that this was "like a mini-grand jury hearing, only I'm the grand jury."

The relational nature of power comes through in complaint procedures such as these. Moving from "listening subject . . . [to] speaking subject,"[31] from spectator/umpire to inquisitor/counsellor, the clerk was most powerful when he could simultaneously occupy "local" space and "legal" space, so that he could use his authority as an official of the state to privilege a definition of events that "made sense" to complainants and others. In some hearings, the clerk's "externality" precluded this form of empowerment, while in others, collective actions undermined his capacity to engage local knowledge effectively. In addition, as I argue in the next chapter, clerks differ in their capacity to mobilize power, and court policy affects their options in doing so.

The perception that citizens who bring complaints are turning to "the courthouse people" to realize a diffuse set of rights constitutes the courthouse as a forum where the "common" sense of gender, of race, and of class can be challenged and reproduced in hearings about "harassment," "trespassing," "threats," "assault," or "disturbing the peace." The relatively cursory denial of most complaints at the Essex court, in hearings that tended to emphasize what was *not* criminal about the experiences that brought complainants to the courthouse, led some to conclude, as one frustrated woman said after a hearing, that they had "no rights at all." For these people, complaining reproduced their experience of powerlessness in hearings where counselling displaced entitlement.[32]

In Franklin County, where strategies of dismissal were more subtle, this sense of powerlessness was diminished. Clerks used "technical issuances" that "held complaints at the show cause level" to obtain consent from complainants for outcomes that were "short" of issuance but that implied recognition of the legitimacy of their complaint. At this court, more experienced parties sometimes took over the hearing, incorporating the show cause procedure into their own histories of struggle; and the clerks' skill in shaping the meanings of trouble through the intimacy of little chats could be matched by the ingenuity of parties in interpreting the meanings of crime. Thus, hearings in Franklin County were powerful local arenas, where the experience of entitlement was created in the potential space for maneuver between trouble and crime.[33]

The difference between these two courts is developed in more detail in the following chapter, in which I examine variations in the subtle interplay of official power with local knowledge, and variation in the kinds of authority produced by embedding one in the other. Each of the clerks interprets his role as gatekeeper somewhat differently, as shaped by his own background, professional aspirations, and the constraints imposed by the particular court in which he practices. At the same time, they all reproduce a juridical field in which the distinction between "court" and "community," or between what belongs "upstairs" and "downstairs" is paradigmatic, although each of them reveals the contradictions of this division in slightly different ways.[34] In this sense, different clerks are "made" by different courts, just as the clerks, embodying different kinds of common sense about the place of law in the everyday, produce slightly different worlds out of the conflicts brought to them by complainants.

CHAPTER 5

RELATIONSHIPS AND THE PRACTICE OF PEACEMAKING

"A lot of it is, people want to come to the courthouse. That keeps things out of court. They need a third party and they don't have one available."

Assistant Clerk Magistrate,
Franklin County

This chapter examines local variations on a common cultural theme in the management of family and neighbor trouble in criminal complaint hearings. Complaints brought by citizens to the court clerks at the Franklin County District Court in Greenfield and the District Court of Essex in Salem are viewed and managed as "garbage cases," matter that is "out of place"[1] in a court that enforces the criminal law. This is a familiar pattern in courts across the nation, and is part of a complex process in which the creation of centers and margins in law, and the privileging of property transactions and property crime over the "interpersonal," produces a hierarchy of courts, and a hierarchy within courts, that is marked by the people, the spaces, and the times that are assigned to "garbage."[2]

If garbage is seen primarily as a marker of boundaries, separating the vulgar from the professional business of law,[3] then it is at these boundaries, and specifically in their construction as boundaries, that the interdependence of law and of "not law" becomes most clear and the distinctions constituted by garbage most clearly arbitrary. By contrasting the increasing marginalization of the "interpersonal" as a subject for mediation at the Essex court, with the more integral place of family and neighbor complaints in Franklin County, I suggest how the juridical field is organized and produced in the everyday practice of these institutions.

STEREOTYPED DISMISSALS:
"THERE'S NO SUCH CRIME" IN ESSEX

There are three clerks at the District Court of Essex, but only one of them regularly attends to citizen complaints.[4] James McGuire, an Irish Catholic and a Salem native, is a wiry, gray-haired man in his fifties who was employed for several years as a filing clerk at the court before his promotion to Assistant Clerk Magistrate. The other two clerks at this court, better educated and more articulate than he, are responsible for managing the official criminal caseload and performing regular clerical functions in the criminal court; only occasionally do they preside at show cause hearings. McGuire, by contrast, makes his way into criminal court only when he is not required for traffic and citizen matters.

The division of labor between clerks at this court indicates both the low status of the junior clerk and how complaints by private citizens are perceived. Staff in the clerk's office describe citizen complaints as "the shit cases," and explain: "We don't have time to deal with personal and neighborhood disputes. . . . [T]his 'he-touched-me' . . . stuff. [We] shouldn't have to mess with that." And the Clerk Magistrate at the court notes, "He [McGuire] loves them . . . but I've got better things for him to do." In the view of the Clerk Magistrate, stories of physical threat and physical violence belong in mediation, although he concedes that "If you come in here with two shiners, you shouldn't have to put up with that."

At this court, the marginalization of complaints by private citizens is represented in the development of a court-based mediation program that is regarded as a model for out of court settlement of conflict. Mediators, who are recruited from surrounding communities, come regularly to the clerk's office to choose cases they will handle, while judges refer other cases directly to the program.[5] There was widespread perception at this court that interpersonal cases (complaints of "assault," "threats," "harassment," and the like) would increasingly be sent to the program, a practice that was transforming show cause hearings into an arena for what court staff considered "the routine" ("larceny by check," "welfare fraud," and so forth).[6]

In this context, McGuire's self professed preference for the "interpersonal" affirmed his marginality at the Essex court. Originally assigned to him because others had "better things to do," neighbor and family conflicts are the source of his satisfaction as a court official. "A and B, harassment, threats—they're the interesting cases. There's a challenge! You can really help people."[7] By contrast, the growing predominance of what he refers to as "checks and DPW" make for a complaint practice that he describes as "boring."[8] As a result, McGuire was particularly concerned about court policy encouraging the referral of citizen complaints to the mediation program.[9] As mediation personnel began appearing regularly in the clerk's office to look through complaint applications for those that seemed appropriate for mediation, he worried that "It's not going to be worth coming here anymore!"

The increasing compartmentalization of what are regarded as "noncriminal" cases at the Essex court is both a function of its place as the home court of the Chief Justice of Massachusetts District Courts, and of caseload pressures connected to its location within the urban sprawl of the greater Boston area. The bulk of the official criminal caseload at this court consists of motor-vehicle complaints brought by state police.[10] Like citizen complaints, these are also handled by the Clerk Magistrate, but are given priority in scheduling and are allotted a greater proportion of hearing time each day.[11] In addition, local businesses use complaint hearings before the clerk as a collection procedure. This function is also given priority over nonproperty complaints by citizens.[12] Finally, government agencies (Department of Public Welfare, Board of Health, the fire department, school department) bring frequent complaints of nonsupport, of welfare fraud, and of code violations of various kinds.[13] Some of these, such as nonsupport and welfare fraud cases, resemble private collection cases in that they require the court's authority in arranging a schedule of payment.

The transformation of the complaint procedure into a debt collection function at the Essex court resembles early twentieth-century efforts to replace magistrates' courts with administrative agencies.[14] Similarly, referring citizen complaints to mediation is one dimension of the widespread contemporary professional move to delegalize minor criminal matters.[15] This elaboration of the juridical field in Essex as spheres of bounded interests and needs, some legal, some administrative, and some therapeutic, has been shaped by the position of this court as a paradigm of a fully "professional" institution, and is in keeping with its place as the home court of the Chief Justice of Massachusetts District Courts, who has sought to embody at his institution the goals of Progressive and later advocates of court reform.

As a consequence, there is relatively little scope for peacemaking in the complaint procedure at the Essex court. In spite of this constraint, the Assistant Clerk attempts to combine dismissal of citizen complaints with some form of mediation. To accomplish this, he underscores the differences between crime and troubles brought to him by complainants. His inflexibility in this regard is often frustrating to those who appear before him, but in his own view he is both protecting himself from ridicule by those "upstairs" *and* is providing a clientele for his own activities as peacemaker. His authority as peacemaker is undermined, however, by his apparent powerlessness in manipulating the law.

Sitting behind a cluttered desk in a small office, McGuire typically asks complainants to begin by reading their own application. Drawing then on the words used by complainants to frame a charge, he shapes a response in terms that emphasize technicalities of procedure and definition. "I can't issue on the assault because you didn't go to the hospital right away," he explained to one irate complainant; and, as we have seen, complainants who filed for harassment were told "There's no such crime."[16]

McGuire's repeated insistence that "no judge is going to hear" these cases, that "the judge" or "Rogers" [the Clerk Magistrate] would "throw it out," or that "we can't take up court time with this," sets an official limit to what he perceives as the "legal" part of a show cause hearing, while justifying his own efforts at settlement following dismissal of a complaint. Uninterested in questions of entitlement, and convinced, like his superiors, that most complaints brought by citizens are *not* "legal" matters, he moves hurriedly toward a dismissal so that he can focus on what most concerns him: healing breaches in relationship through lectures about parental duties, the virtues of shaking hands, and the inappropriateness of violence between friends or intimates. As the hearing proceeds, however, he is frequently interrupted by the telephone or by secretaries looking for documents on his desk. Thus his efforts to mediate conflicts are complicated by fragmented hearings, carried out under pressure from others in the office who indicate openly that this activity is a waste of time.

Uneasily positioned between the court proper, which he refers to as "upstairs," and the mediation program on the floor below him, McGuire continually struggles to establish his authority over the flow of cases in either direction. To disgruntled complainants, he explains his failure to issue complaints by relying on technicalities and by likening his stance to that of a truly "legal" judge ("no judge is going to hear this case"), even as he confirms his own relative powerlessness with a comment like "the judge would think I was crazy if I sent this upstairs." By relying on technicalities, this clerk gives "an increasingly authoritative and neutral character to [his] . . . arguments," as Bourdieu has noted in a discussion of semiprofessional mediators, but does so "at the risk of undermining the very logic of the process of amicable negotiation to begin with."[17] In this way, he contributes to a process of juridicization that has marginalized lay people, and that is transforming mediation itself into a "neutral" process, involving mediators who bring a detached stance to their practice.[18]

By contrast to McGuire's confident assertion of control over complaints that should not go "upstairs," the movement of cases to the mediation program was a constant source of aggravation to him, since his experience was of having *no* control over the activities of mediators: "I think I should be able to decide what goes downstairs. . . . I think I can look at them and decide whether or not to have a hearing." He experienced the increasingly regular visits by mediators to the clerk's office as acts of appropriation and the exchanges and tensions over who should handle citizen complaints contributed to his tenuous identity as the official peacemaker who could "help people."

The reiteration in complaint hearings of the division between "upstairs" and "downstairs" at this court, the division of labor between the clerks, with the least educated responsible for "interpersonal" (or "garbage") and "collection" cases, and the struggles over control of complaints perceived as appropriate for mediation, are all part of the production of the juridical field at the Essex court, constituting specific "interests" and "needs" in connection with specialized procedures and professionals who operate in the shadow of the law. These "needs," in turn, and the agents who fulfill them, are explainable only in the context of the distinction they establish between official and informal, or professional and lay, practice.

At the Franklin County court, by contrast, the connection of the local and the lay to "garbage" has more ambiguous connotations. Here, resistance to the centralization of law and the marginalization and disempowerment of rural courts is in tension with the professional aspirations of court staff. "Garbage" cases encode local political contests and provide a vehicle for domesticating the law. At the same time, their segregation in "private" show cause hearings signifies the disengagement of the court from these contests, and the professional legitimacy this disengagement implies. The ambiguity surrounding garbage cases in Franklin County is captured in the Assistant Clerk's observation that "People want to come to the courthouse; that keeps things out of court."

"TECHNICAL ISSUANCE": BETWEEN MORALITY AND LAW IN FRANKLIN COUNTY

Like Essex, court staff in Franklin County describe family and neighbor cases as "garbage," and the people who bring them as "brainless." At the same time, "garbage" cases in Franklin County are defined (by the presiding justice at this court) as "little problems" that need "to be heard," so people "don't take it into their own hands if they can't resolve them." This approach stems, in part, from the close ties of court staff to town in Greenfield, ties that the two presiding judges experience as linking them to working class citizens.

The presiding justice (John O'Malley) was raised in what he describes as "mostly a railroad community" on the outskirts of Greenfield proper, locally known as "Bingville." His family moved there as his father, who was on the "spare board," gradually worked his way up the railway line and acquired seniority. This judge still has ties with people in Bingville, joining schoolmates from that neighborhood at high school reunions. He became a practicing lawyer in the 1950s and served in the state legislature for 12 years before being appointed judge in the mid-1970s.

The other judge assigned to the court (Jeffrey Miller), and the assistant clerk (Gabriel LeBlanc), also grew up on what they describe as "the other side of the tracks" in Greenfield. Miller, whose father owned a small grocery store, became a partner in a local law firm and served on the board of one of Greenfield's major financial institutions before his appointment to the bench. LeBlanc is a former town policeman. Others at the court also have strong ties to the town of Greenfield, where most were born or raised, and where many belong to social clubs such as Moose, Elks, Rotary, or the golf club. One of the administrative assistants in the clerk's office is the daughter of a former Greenfield police chief. Many court employees are active in local churches, where they continue to socialize with people they know from high school and their neighborhoods. They share the working class background of the people who appear in court as complainants, victims, or defendants.

The experienced connection of court staff to court users shapes the perception of clerks and judges that neighbor and family troubles should "be heard." At the same time, their capacity to hear them is influenced by the relatively light criminal caseload at the court, where the number of motor-vehicle complaints is far smaller than in Essex.[19] Not only is the criminal caseload smaller at this court, but the "continuing flow" of cases that the clerks regularly deal with is quite different.[20] This is in part a function of where each court is located (with a greater number of motor-vehicle complaints in the urban sprawl of Boston), but it is also a function of court policy. For example, at the Essex court, larceny-by-check complaints brought by businesses comprise 39% of the cases heard by the clerk,[21] while in Franklin County they make up only 4% of the clerk's caseload.[22] Court policy in Franklin County allows such cases only when a repeat offender is involved, where the issue is not simply one of collection, but of a problem *person*.

These differences in the continuing flow of cases between the two courts shape the skills that clerks in each court are expected (and encouraged) to develop. At the Essex court, the clerk is viewed by other court officials as a collection agent for the routine; his competence is judged by his efficiency in working out schedules of payment for traffic violations and unpaid goods. In Franklin County, by contrast, show cause hearings regulate local morality, with the law as a tool in this process. The clerk frames events as moral, as legal, or as monetary, to persuade the parties to comply. His capacity to do this is, in part, a function of the cases before him (no larceny-by-check, fewer traffic), but it is equally shaped by the place allotted to relational problems at an institution where officials at all levels (from superior court judges to district court clerks) underscore the law's relevance to local culture and politics, transforming "the local" and "the legal" in this process.

While this more complex interpretation of complaint procedure is common to the practice of both Franklin County clerks, each uses somewhat different strategies to control the way the court becomes involved in a particular incident of trouble.[23] "Technical issuance," which recognizes the official legitimacy of a complaint, while keeping it "out of court," is a term used by the Assistant Clerk Magistrate, but it captures the complex ways in which this court becomes caught up in the problems of family and neighborhood life.

Lawrence Simpson, the Clerk Magistrate of the Franklin County District Court, is a restrained and somewhat formal man in his late thirties. His formality extends not only to complaint hearings, where his manner is somewhat detached and his style marked by careful attention to "correct" procedure, but to his relations with co-workers and colleagues at the court, as well. Even though he has been a clerk since 1975, he describes himself as an "outsider" in an office where "almost everyone else is an insider." This identity refers specifically to the fact that he is not "from" Greenfield but grew up in nearby Millers Falls, and presently lives in Deerfield, a town just south of Greenfield.

The son of a mold setter at Millers Falls Machine Company, Simpson describes himself as having "more in common with users of the court than with some of the lawyers, or even some of the police." He is married to an attorney, yet describes his background like other court staff do, "from working class homes originally and still relatively poor economically." Simpson's formal schooling extends considerably beyond that of others in the clerk's office. Although he is not legally trained, he has an undergraduate degree in political science and economics, and a graduate degree in education from the University of Massachusetts.

In spite of the connections he notes between court users and court staff, Simpson distinguishes court users as "overridingly the poor. . . . [T]he consistent pattern is that we are not dealing in criminal court and in show cause with the middle class." These people "look to the court as a final resort" and want it "to resolve all manner of conflicts." As a consequence, Simpson describes complaint hearings as "a forum where you can get more information to see if weeding out is possible."

For Simpson, "weeding out" involves distinguishing between the "technically criminal" (a bad check case, or rocks thrown at someone's car by a child), and

> their purpose when they are applying for a complaint. . . .
> You try to key in on what people say and how they say it.
> What are their goals and objectives in bringing it to a pub-
> lic . . . well, not public . . . but to a hearing? Do they want
> punishment for the adult or for the child? What is their
> hidden agenda?

Almost all hearings at the Franklin County court are held in the juvenile courtroom, where the clerk sits at a raised bench, looking down on other participants. Hearings are recorded and all begin with the same introduction explaining the nature of the proceeding and the rights of the accused to counsel.[24] Simpson's formality extends beyond these features, common to all show cause hearings at this court, in that his manner is relatively impassive. He frames his clarifications in the language of "case" and "statute," and takes his decisions "under advisement" rather than deciding in the charged atmosphere created by the hearing itself. For example, in an assault complaint where the attorney argued for issuance because there had been unpermitted touching, Simpson took the complaint under advisement but denied it a week later, after consulting the Massachusetts General Laws. He justified his denial on the basis that criminal assault requires intent to cause physical harm, "not simply touching with intent."

Even in speaking with relatively young children, Simpson rarely moves far from the discursive space of the law. In a hearing on another assault and battery complaint, this time involving a fight between three 10 year olds on their way to school, Simpson addressed the daughter of the woman who brought the complaint:

> Clerk: Corinne, do you understand the difference between
> right and wrong, and what it means to lie or tell the truth?
> Corinne: Yes.
> Clerk: Do you understand that you are going to be under
> oath to tell the truth today about what happened?

At the conclusion of the hearing, addressing Michael, one of the boys accused of hitting Corinne, the clerk said:

> Clerk: Wait a minute. Do you have any other fellows in your class that are bigger than you?
> Michael: Yes.
> Clerk: Do they aggravate you?
> Michael: No.
> Clerk: Why?
> Michael: Because they're bigger. Well, I get in fights with bigger boys. I got in a fight with Bobby once.
> Clerk: Who won?
> Michael: There were no winners or losers.
> Clerk: There never are, are there? Well, I think there's cause for a complaint, and normally, I might allow it. But they're going to be in school together for a long time. . . . [so] I'm not going to do that. *I'm going to put you on probation with your mother and Mrs. Taylor, in a sense.* If I hear anything from anyone that this kind of thing is going on again, I'll issue a complaint and then you'll have to go to court [emphasis added].

Here the clerk placed familiar metaphors of legal procedure (being "under oath" and being placed "on probation") in everyday moral and relational contexts ("the difference between right and wrong," "on probation with your mother") in an effort both to make "common" sense of law and to extend its authority into everyday situations (mother/child, right/wrong). The clerk's exchange with the boy moved briefly away from events surrounding the complaint to other social experiences he might understand from the perspective of his 10-year-old victim. At the same time, he returned immediately to the notion of a legal context for dealing with the problem, in his reference to putting him on probation with his mother.

Like all of the clerks I observed, Simpson constructed moments of intimacy by going "off the record" during some hearings. He did so as an effort to reach a settlement, pointing out all the while that "if [this case] goes to court, none of the peripheral issues—about noise, disturbances, disagreements—are going to be admitted into evidence." But even "off the record" his advice was framed in legal terms, with references to admissible evidence in a court proceeding, and explicit mention of the record from which he was temporarily departing. In this way, he used legal procedures to maintain control, urging settlement during a hearing as a means of avoiding a less responsive court, or refusing access to the court by comparing the intentions of parties at the hearing with the language of the criminal code.

Although this clerk used the complaint procedure as a mechanism for "weeding out" complaints, he was alert to subtexts in a complainant's story that signaled the need for "a more formal setting." Determining when this point was reached depended on who was involved, as well as on the circumstances (for example, daily fighting in an area, the presence of a weapon, or bodily injury). In particular, he seemed concerned about complaints involving people who "lack a sense of right and wrong and of conforming to community standards,"[25] and this concern emerged in certain racially related neighborhood fights, as well as in complaints involving runaway teenage women. Where runaway teenagers were involved, Simpson occasionally urged complainants to file formal charges and told social workers handling teenage runaways: "Don't hesitate to file complaints in these cases." On the general pattern of older men furnishing younger women with "dope or liquor" in complaints involving runaways, Johnson noted: "I just want to see this change." These complaints, while constituting a relatively small proportion of the show cause caseload,[26] were symbolic, a weathervane of declining morality in Greenfield. Their identification and construction as "crime" at the show cause level marked one of the ways in which hearings regulated local morality, bringing "family" and "community" problems into the legitimate domain of the law.

Gabriel LeBlanc, known to colleagues and townspeople alike as "Gaby," is the Assistant Clerk Magistrate at the Franklin County court. A gray-haired man in his late fifties, he was a Greenfield policeman for 21 years before joining the court staff. He describes this shift in career as "a fluke." After years on the police force, first on foot patrol, then in a cruiser for 10 years, he had moved from night beat, to day beat, and finally to detective, and was not sure where he could go from there. Shortly after the incumbent Assistant Clerk had a heart attack, he sat in her chair one day when he was at the court and "I made a crack about trying it out." A few days later the Clerk Magistrate asked him if he was serious.[27] Gaby recalls, "I'd never thought of it . . . I was thrilled. It was two times the pay of a policeman." With characteristic irony, and referring to recent publicity about the failure of all Greenfield policemen to pass standard qualifying examinations for promotion, he added: "I flatter myself I made the wrong decision. If I'd stayed on I could have passed the tests and I'd be police chief."

Gaby grew up in Greenfield. His father, born in Northampton, was of French-Canadian ancestry; his mother, of German descent, was a native of Greenfield, where her father had immigrated from Silesia at the turn of the century. Three of her brothers became small business-men in Greenfield, where they owned a rug cleaning company which stayed in the family until 1982; a fourth, the father of the present court reporter for the local newspaper, became caretaker for the president of Millers Falls Machine (the same company where the father of the Clerk Magistrate worked as a mold-setter).

Commenting only briefly on his own upbringing, Gaby remarked in a conversation about neighborhoods that "I can't tell you much about that because I moved around so much." While frequent moves as a child gave him no personal ties with Greenfield neighborhoods, his experience as a policeman meant that he was keenly attuned to dis-tinctions of class and of place in the town. High Street, Highland Avenue, and Converse were metonyms for the established community of bankers and business people, while reference to North Parish, Four Corners, and Federal Street suggested the more modest life-style and working class background of families such as his own. Observing that "people go where they belong," he responded to my request that he elaborate: "If you were my wife and we were going out on a Saturday night, I wouldn't take you to Ray's Cafe." Ray's Cafe, known as a local "trouble spot," is where "a class of people" go.[28]

Gaby's detailed knowledge of people and places in Greenfield is one of his key attributes as clerk. Estimating that he knows at least 50% of those who appear before him at the court, he speculated once on whether he would "be the same clerk" if he were put in another court, for example in Boston, or in Salem. "Could I do the same job?," he asked reflectively, suggesting by his tone that he could not. In Greenfield, the middle class complainant who comes to him because "he used to bust me when I was a teenager," the alcoholic who has faced him on repeated complaints of disturbing the peace, and the transient who lumbers regularly into the courthouse or a church cof-fee hour demanding advice and reassurance, all accept his judgment and counsel. His intimate acquaintance with local persons, places, and histories enables him to situate events in particular settings and suggest solutions that reflect local expectations. In this way he avoids an overtly coercive role while defining events and relationships in terms of his own concerns about morality and order.

An example of this is Gaby's handling of a complaint brought by a retired working class man from Deerfield, a town a few miles to the south of Greenfield.[29] The complaint was framed as an "assault" in which the retired man claimed that the owner of a motorcycle business next door had "poked" him. Gaby responded to this allegation that there was no "real" assault involved because "You weren't hurt. There was no hospitalization, and you weren't really threatened. So that's not the problem." Rather, as the answers to his questions gradually revealed, the problem was one of noise, created when the businessman allowed customers to test motorcycles on the track behind his store. The complainant had taken the problem to town meeting, and had called the police several times, but the noise had continued. On the day of the poking incident, he said, "I just kept hearing that awful noise. . . . He's going around and around the track and it just got on my nerves."

Both parties agreed that the "real" problem in this complaint was the motorcycle noise, but the businessman suggested that this was no more a problem than other noises accompanying local industry: "Where I live in Whately, I have a nice home in farm country. When they harvest tobacco, there's three generators going all night long. But what am I going to do about it? Complain that they're disturbing the peace?" The clerk, however, responded that "that's the way of life in Whately. You could move down to New York City and there'd be nothing you could do about the noise either. He was living there quietly before the motorcycle shop moved in." Gaby explained to the complainant that he could issue a complaint for "disturbing the peace"; but he suggested instead an agreement where the businessman would limit testing on the track, and would fence the area so he had better control over its use. When the businessman said "I . . . feel like *I'm* the one being picked on. It's *my* property!," the clerk responded, "There's a limit to things you can do on your property."

Building on his experience as a policeman, Gaby describes his approach to citizen complaints as "playing it by ear." Like a policeman, he does "what you think will work."

> They [the parties] come here because they want to drag the other one into court. It doesn't matter if it's a clerk or a judge. . . . When I went to the police academy, one of my teachers there said that if we went back . . . and did everything as it was written in the books, we might as well never leave the police station. . . . If the law is over here [indicating an imaginary space to his left] and morality is over here [indicating a space to his right], the middle area between them is where I want to stay. Sometimes I'll move as far as possible to one side or the other in order to accomplish what I need to.

One of his strategies for accomplishing this movement between law and morality is the concept of "technical issuance." Technical issuance recognizes the legitimacy of a complaint as a legal or criminal matter, but "holds" the complaint "at the show cause level." That is, the complaint remains a "private" disturbance, but is available for issuance if there is "more trouble" from the person complained against. This is similar to a continuance, a form of disposition used in both Franklin County and in Essex,[30] with the crucial difference, however, that the distinction between quarrel and crime is not spelled out in a technical issuance. For example, in an "assault and battery" complaint brought by Jane Bailey, a woman in her fifties who was the co-owner of a package store in a town near Greenfield, against George Green, who owned the store with her, Gaby concluded: "There's good reason for a complaint to issue right now." Instead of issuing the complaint, however, he told Green he was "like on probation. You'll have to be on your best behavior. If she comes in with another complaint, we'll issue the other one forthwith—then you'll have two complaints. So that'll give you something to think about."

In other complaints, Gaby used the language of morality more than of law to control the hearing. For example, in a Greenfield complaint brought by the father of an 8 year old against a 14 year old living on an adjacent street, the complainant alleged that the older boy had damaged his son's "Big Wheels" toy:

> I went to call for my son to come home, and he didn't come so I walked down Pine Street. Joe and Tommy, they come up with the Big Wheels, but they couldn't ride, the wheels were twisted in an L. I got home and I asked Tommy what happened to the Big Wheels, and he said Joe got on, and then made Tommy push him, and then Joe took it and threw it across the street. This isn't the first time.

Gaby called Tommy up to the bench after his father had spoken, and asked him what happened. Tommy responded that "Joe broke it." As the hearing proceeded, there was some disagreement about whether the Big Wheels had been broken before Joe rode it, and there was talk about other incidents in which Joe had smashed Tommy's belongings. Finally, Gaby commented to Tommy's father: "He's a bit young to be playing with a fourteen-year-old." When the man responded that "He's not out of my sight for long," Gaby retorted: "If you're at 134 [Mayfield Street] and he's over there on Pine, he's out of your sight. The wrong guy comes cruisin' along, he's gonna be goin' for a ride. There's not much evidence to issue a complaint." Here, the clerk's familiarity with the neighborhood provided the context for his transformation of a criminal complaint into a moral lapse, this time on the part of the complainant.

In this case, like the complaint about the motorcycle noise, the clerk's detailed local knowledge provided him with "personalized and far-reaching control."[31] He was not insensitive to rights claims in some cases, remarking, for example, that for the motorcycle shop owner, "It's a tough thing. He's trying to run a business down there, and his neighbors are all upset because of the noise." But he intuitively placed claims of rights in a broader relational context, observing (as he did in the following comment to a teenager in another complaint about motorcycle noise):

> The only thing I can say is you've got to learn to be considerate of your neighbors. Being friends with your neighbors is a good thing. You've got to live with them. . . . It's not that simple. We're in a society of people, and what you do is other people's business, because it affects them. . . . That reminds me of a story. All these people were in a lifeboat, and one guy's huddled down there in a corner, and he won't have anything to do with anybody. All of the time he was saying 'It's none of your business what I'm doing,' but he was steadily digging a hole in the bottom.

In a third hearing, Angela Sokia, a woman from Turners Falls, brought a complaint of "disturbing the peace" against Danny Gagne, a man from the same town whom she claimed had been yelling obscene remarks at her. Here, Gaby implicitly used the "lifeboat" philosophy (that "what you do is other people's business"), but in this case it became the basis for *issuing* the complaint. After hearing a witness confirm Angela's story that Danny yelled "Who're you going to blow next? You're nothing but an old slut!" as she walked up the street in Turners Falls, Gaby said that there was enough evidence to allow her application. Before doing so, however, he turned to Angela and asked "Is that what you want to have happen?" When she agreed, he set a date for the arraignment in criminal court.

In this case, the clerk's view of the complaint was shaped by increasing concerns (voiced in the media and elsewhere) about problems with loiterers in Turners Falls, where they were accused by merchants and police of discouraging customers with their comments and disruptive behavior. Thus the complainant's interest in stopping the defendant's persistent harassment coincided with official concerns about the effects of such incidents on local businesses, shaping the perception of the incident as a matter of concern to the court, rather than simply as a typical "garbage case." Following Gaby's issuance of the complaint application, the case was settled with a guilty finding in court and payment of a $50 fine by the defendant.

Unlike the head clerk at this court, who was more likely to object to what he once termed "ridiculous" complaints, the Assistant Clerk was philosophical about what he viewed as "problems that will never be solved." He did not discourage complaints about neighborhood "feuds" and "lovers' quarrels," using hearings on these matters as a sounding board and as a place for advising people who "want to come to the courthouse."

As "third party," he alternately lectured, counselled, and ridiculed participants in a hearing, relying on his personal authority as much as on the law to accomplish particular ends. He was as likely to admonish fighting neighbors that "if you had any brains, you would stay away from each other," as to counsel an alcoholic that he was not "crazy. . . . Just can't see the forest because the trees got in the way."

While Gaby did not hesitate to overrule the protests of complainants who disagreed with his judgment, or to silence belligerent defendants with the remark that "This is like a grand jury hearing. Only I'm the grand jury," he more typically sought to include complainants in a decision to dismiss, as in the case above. "Well, what do you want me to do?," he would ask as a way of bringing to a close a hearing in which he had subtly but carefully built up to the only outcome which would "make sense." In such hearings, decisions emerged from a joint process of give-and-take, with the clerk working through or building on the narratives of the parties to construct an account that would produce an outcome *he* considered appropriate.

At the Essex court, the disorder of complaint hearings, and their location "below" the formal arena of law, is part of the practical activity of worldmaking that sets the domain of law apart from the practices of a lay clerk. The clerk constructs this separate world of law in hearings that repeatedly distinguish the problems before him from those that belong before a judge, but in doing so replicates the process that Bourdieu has termed "juridicization." In Franklin County, by contrast, the formality of the complaint procedure, and the practical skill of the clerks (particularly of the Assistant Clerk) in moving easily between the vulgar and the professional visions of a case,[32] constructs a more ambiguous legal/social world, one in which, for example "threat to commit a crime *is* a crime and it *isn't* a crime," depending on the clerk's interpretations of whether specific actions constitute "threat." This, in turn, is dependent on *his* understanding of local lifeways, his connections to those who live them, and his sense of whether a finding of probable cause makes political and moral sense in the context of local politics and local moralities.

The absence at the Franklin County court of a clear distinction between legal and local problems, or between governance and judicial functions, is the source of the "gentle violence" with which the force of law takes hold in the lives of citizens who "choose" their own dismissals in hearings before the Assistant Clerk,[33] in this way obscuring the dependence of these "choices" on his capacity for persuasion. The clerk's persuasive capacity, however, is a function of his ties to local people and his embeddedness in local problems. His power to "manipulate legal aspirations" by "revealing rights . . . and revealing injustices"[34] is contingent, characterized, like the juridical field itself, "by an independence achieved in and through dependence."[35]

Two dimensions of this interdependence need further exploration. In Chapter 6, I return to a theme touched on in Chapter 4, that of the ways in which the local embeddedness of court staff in Franklin County creates a potential space for invention in complaint hearings. By examining a series of complaints brought to the court clerk from the town of Turners Falls I focus on how low income complainants construct themselves within the discursive space of the law, appropriating the law in ways that disrupt its use by state officials to control them. In Chapter 7, I move away from the clerk to examine the construction of a neighborhood quarrel as a transgression of property rights by affluent complainants in Franklin County, who sued in Superior Court to prevent the development of a local hill by new neighbors. This chapter again suggests, although in very different ways than Chapter 6, how "private" matters can be transformed into collective struggles in contests where the law itself becomes "a permanently available site of contested meanings."[36]

"KIDSTUFF" AT THE COURTHOUSE

The actual order of things is precisely what "popular" tactics turn to their own ends, without any illusion that it will change any time soon. Though elsewhere it is exploited by a dominant power or simply denied by an ideological discourse, here order is *tricked* by an art.

Michel de Certeau,
The Practice of Everyday Life, 1984

This chapter examines neighbor conflicts brought to the Franklin County court from Turners Falls, a town with a large population of welfare recipients who are clients of Greenfield's social service agencies. The chapter explores how complainants from Turners Falls deploy legal concepts of crime to demand their entitlement to safety, to shelter, and to justice, thereby constructing themselves as disruptive subjects whose disorderly lives require a paternalistic court. By involving the court in their struggles, unruly complainants whose "way of life is fighting"[1] domesticate the law; at the same time, these fights become a critical vantage point from which "the law" (and the white, middle class order this represents) can be interpreted by court staff, as distinct from the chaotic lives of people who occasionally undermine this order in court.

In developing this argument, I return to my earlier discussion of power as a relationship, and of governance as the exercise of power by agents who "lastingly 'bind' each other" through the "inevitably interested relations" of kinship, family, and community.[2] The mutual dependence of clerks and parties to complaints makes possible the governance of parties by the clerk, just as it makes possible the domestication of law by disruptive subjects from Turners Falls. Historian Michel de Certeau describes what I term "domestication" as "'putting it over' on the established order on its home ground" by "insinuating" into the court an "esthetics of 'tricks'" and an "ethics of tenacity (countless ways of refusing to accord the established order the status of a law, a meaning, or a fatality)."[3] Complainants juxtapose discordant ways of telling or doing (the distortion of a familiar story line, play with conventional time and space arrangements, the unfamiliar positioning of actors vis-à-vis one another) with conventional practices and forms, engaging others at the court in these alternative tellings and constituting the court itself as a site of insurgency, however temporary.

In describing the aesthetics of tricks and the ethics of tenacity at the Franklin County court, I focus on two histories. The first involves a homeless man whose familiarity with the court system and long-term relations with court staff allowed him to turn the law against itself by engaging clerks and judges in a mockery of court procedure. The second involves neighbors in Turners Falls whose complaints made them objects of surveillance by the court, but whose frequent appearances became a way of subverting official procedure as they converted "private" hearings into public battlegrounds, transforming the court itself in the process. I begin with the story of "Charlie," then move in the second part of the chapter to a description of historical and contemporary social and economic issues in Turners Falls, as these shape the management of complaints in court, and to a discussion of "A Bad Neighborhood" from which these complaints emerge.

"CHARLIE"

"Charlie" was an infamous courthouse regular, familiar to clerks, judges, and probation staff, and a constant source of aggravation to police. Listed officially as "of no known address," he was known in Greenfield as the man from the Renaissance Church, a commune that had been active in Turners Falls since the 1970s and continued to own property in that town in the 1980s. Reputed to have come from a "wealthy New York family," "Charlie" had been in and out of mental institutions for years, and was said to have destroyed his life with LSD. At the court, his actions were viewed with an uneasy mixture of tolerance and fear, as his antics transformed trials and complaint hearings into parodies of the legal process, implicating court officials and local citizens in his own self-conscious mockery of law.

Well over six feet tall, and weighing perhaps 300 pounds, Charlie clothed himself in a bizarre assemblage: top hat, soiled white shirt, and baggy pants that drooped far below his waist. With a stomach that bulged beyond his shirt, Charlie always overflowed the space he occupied, belching continuously, and commenting on court procedures in a loud, belligerent manner. His erratic behavior on the street and in court—variously interpreted as nuisance, disturbance, or crime—was in marked contrast to his mastery of bargaining in court—often thought to be reserved for attorneys rather than indigents. Part lawyer, part street person, Charlie connected through his actions and dress the key distinctions on which the identity of Greenfield's middle class was created: its capacity for moderation and self-control, as versus "the other half of America" whose life of "fighting" was a continual affirmation of uncontrolled passion.[4]

Court staff were both wary and tolerant of Charlie's performances. They were a familiar routine which broke the monotony of less colorful proceedings; but they were also a way of tracking the potential danger he was seen to represent for the community at large.[5] Earlier court appearances became the predictable "ground" against which the "new" (as dangerous) could emerge in later hearings.[6] At the same time, familiarity with his style made it possible to interpret his actions as ironic commentary, rather than as danger, just as it was Charlie's familiarity with court officials and court procedure that made possible the critique of local justice embedded in his parody of the court. His performances were compelling (and thus permitted) precisely because they spoke to the concerns of *court staff* about the gap between moral and legal sense, and to the limitations of law as a "wet noodle," unable to fully contain the "undesirables" who regularly spilled over into Greenfield, taunting the model of civility it represented. As the Assistant Clerk observed, "The problem is, we've got all these people walking around with all these rights—and some people just shouldn't have them." Noting that "the ones that make the laws are lawyers; the ones who figure out how to get around the laws are lawyers; the judges are lawyers—they're all lawyers!," he suggested the ambiguous potential of law, its lack of a fixed anchoring point, and its openness to meanings that subvert the "moral sense" of local knowledge.

Charlie appeared at the courthouse—on charges ranging from disturbing the peace, to trespassing, to indecent exposure, and finally to indecent assault and battery on a child under 14—at least six times during my research. The following sequence is illustrative of his exchange with the court clerk during one complaint hearing on a charge of exposing himself. The complaint was brought by the Montague Chief of Police, who explained that the incident occurred at a softball game where Charlie, who was standing by the foul line, dropped his pants.

Chief: Officer K. was playing in the game. He told Charlie to leave the park. He wasn't arrested at the time because Officer K. was off-duty.

Charlie: What happened that day. . . . I was just walking down the right field side line. Then the ball came that way. It went just to the left of Officer K., exactly like it was hit for me. No one was going after it, so I just took five or ten steps to get the ball; and as I ran to get the ball, my pants fell down. Wait a minute! I think they fell down after I picked up the ball. . . . My pants fit loosely.

Clerk: Are these the same yellow pants that were the subject of [another hearing]?

Charlie: Yes. First of all, it's totally absurd. . . . Second of all, with my reputation . . . I'd be a fool to pull down my pants in front of a cop who's playing first base. Number three: My pants were only down for a second or two. I pulled them back up as soon as I could.

Clerk: Officer K. didn't arrest you then?

Charlie: No. . . . And number four: Out of three or four hundred people, most of the people thought it was very funny. They wouldn't think it was funny if I did it on purpose. And number five: I was charged with the same offense three weeks ago, and I went to court in front of Judge . . . , and he put $300 bail on me. I'm supposed to be innocent until proven guilty, but having no money, I had to go to jail for 13 days.

Clerk: We're getting a little afield here.

Chief: After the first [complaint], Charlie, you got red suspenders, which you wore all the time.

Charlie: I wore those suspenders for about a week, and my shoulders started to hurt, so I took them off.

This complaint was dismissed by the clerk on grounds that "It isn't so much that I believe everything you said, but I suppose it's possible that what you say is true."

Charlie was not always intent on gaining a dismissal. In court appearances before a judge, he was particularly skillful in using the discourse of rights to secure unorthodox and advantageous sentences. During one appearance in court, following his arrest for an incident at the police station in which he had threatened to urinate on the floor, he bargained openly with the judge for a $25 bail (which he could not afford) and a one-week sentence in jail, so that he could shower and have some meals. Explaining to the judge that a two-week sentence

would be "too long" to confine him with other inmates, he successfully negotiated a disposition that removed him from the street, while
assuring his continued existence as a street person. These negotiations,
repeatedly disrupted by the laughter of a full courtroom, transformed
the hearing into satire in a performance in which Charlie, rather than
the judge, was momentarily in control.

As the most visible and articulate of several well-known figures from
downstreet Turners Falls who more or less openly defied the order of the
court, Charlie embodied the capacity of people "living without social
resources and without trust" to control the law, creating disorder at the
very heart of order.[7] While others stole night sticks from police cars,
"willfully" injured public property by carving their names on courtroom
benches, kicked the courthouse door during a conference with attorneys,
or spit on the floor of the courtroom during a private complaint hearing,
Charlie's defiance was always enacted in public, intended as performance and interpreted as entertainment by onlookers.

Even as they laughed at his antics, however, court staff commented
on the threatening subtext in Charlie's actions. No one was surprised
when he was arrested for climbing the fire escape outside a child's win-
dow one night to pull the blankets off her as she slept. This incident
was followed by a chaotic series of appearances at the Franklin County
Superior Court in which he refused the counsel of a court-appointed
attorney, insisting that he was competent to represent himself. In a trial
that attracted widespread local media attention, Charlie was described
as he summarized his case to the jury, "speaking to them and eating at
the same time" in a parody of professional behavior. This culminated
in his forcible removal from the courtroom when he tried to speak during the judge's instructions to the jury. Judged competent to stand trial
and guilty as charged, Charlie was given a sentence of 7 to 10 years at
Walpole State Prison and thus indefinitely removed from the streets of
both Greenfield and Turners Falls.[8]

This story, which interweaves an "esthetic of tricks" with individual tragedy, points to the contradictions and the ambiguities of cases
brought to the court from Turners Falls. Straddling an uneasy boundary between "kidstuff" and serious crime, complaints from Turners
inevitably seem to have the potential for both, and thus the parties
involved are both humored and watched by court staff. In hearings
before the clerk, their actions are implicitly contrasted to an ideal of
restrained adult behavior, a contrast embedded in a system of distinctions in which lower class persons and lower class trouble are set apart
from the life style and self-construction of Greenfield's middle class citizens.[9] The most persistent refrain of the Assistant Clerk in show cause

hearings was one of self-control, and of the connections between lack of selfcontrol and lack of civility:

> "Here's a good rule. If you think you're mad enough to fight, think twice. Put your hands in your pockets and walk away. We have to advise husbands to do that when they get mad at their wives. . . . If you want to bring the city—the way they live in the ghettos—to Turners Falls, then keep it up."

Here, Turners Falls is contrasted to "the ghettos," but on other occasions it *is* the ghetto: "This is 1982 and we're supposed to be civilized," the clerk observed in a dispute between two women from Turners Falls. "The law says you can't punch someone in the nose unless you're attacked." In references such as these, Turners Falls, "the ghettos," and "the city" became metaphors for the excess, lack of moderation, and lack of civilization of "the other half of America."[10]

Concerns about the deterioration of Turners Falls into a "slum" were a topic of extensive coverage in the local newspapers during the early 1980s, and were also reflected in complaints of neighborhood fighting brought to the court clerk from the downtown area of Turners during that time. The fighting, much of which had explicit or implicit racial dimensions, coincided with the development of a low-income housing project in Turners Falls, and with concerns about how this project would reshape the character of neighborhood life.

"POWER TOWN"

Turners Falls, first settled in the eighteenth century, was developed a century later by Fitchburg industrialist Alvah Crocker, who made plans for "a great city" at the waterfalls there. In 1869, Greenfield's major employer, a cutlery manufacturer, moved to the town. From the late nineteenth to the early twentieth centuries, Turners expanded with the arrival of English, Irish, German, French-Canadian, and finally Polish immigrants to work in its machine factories and paper mills.[11] Many of these factories failed during the Depression, but paper manufacturing continued to provide a livelihood for the descendants of immigrants, who created a vibrant and heterogeneous cultural life centered on religious societies and neighborhood churches: St. Anne's Parish, known today as the "French Church"; the St. Kazimierz Society, which founded a Polish parish, Our Lady of Czenstochowa Church; and St. Mary's Catholic Church. The ethnicity that shaped and was fostered by these parishes is apparent in the propensity of Turners Falls residents to describe themselves in ethnic terms; but today the town is segmented less by ethnicity than by class, as the working class descendants of nineteenth-century French and Polish laborers moved from "downstreet" tenements that housed factory workers to "the hill," which rises immediately above and to the south. Bounded by large and comfortable houses that set the downstreet section apart, "the hill" extends southeast over a large plain covered with small tidy homes, symmetrical yards, and neatly laid out neighborhood blocks. It is here, according to a successful businessman who grew up in the "downstreet" area, that "the real" Turners Falls people live. People in the downstreet area, by contrast, "are transients, they're on welfare. They aren't like other people."

Downstreet Turners is an area of about six blocks that is occupied by a heterogeneous population. It includes elderly, who are typically retired employees of one of the mills and have lived there all their lives, as well as younger families, single mothers with children, some employed but many on welfare, who live as tenants in buildings owned by absentee landlords. These welfare families may have lived in the area for years, but move frequently due to vagaries of income or state rules that legislate the spatial requirements of families with a particular number, and sexual distribution, of children.[12] Recent gentrification has also brought in residential property owners, young professionals, and working-class families who have purchased homes. Finally, there is a population defined locally as "transient," "of no known address," and "undesirable," and that includes outpatients from a nearby mental hospital, as well as what one court officer described as "hoodlums" and "druggies." Unemployment in the area is high, incomes are generally low, and relatively few people are homeowners.[13]

Until the early 1980s, the downstreet area was dominated by run down tenements, but developers began replacing these with low-income housing in 1981 and 1982. Working collaboratively with a Boston-based management firm, and subsidized with Federal ("Section 8") rent subsidies, one developer, Thomas Judd, transformed 10 vacant or deteriorating buildings on Avenue A and on Fourth and Fifth streets into a modern apartment complex known as the Power Town Apartments.

Power Town, a $4.7 million renovation project, was part of a "revitalization" of downtown Turners Falls,[14] celebrated by state and local officials as converting a "horrendous" area into something in which local people could have "building pride."[15] This revitalization engaged developers from as far away as California, but media attention focused on Thomas Judd, a Turners Falls native and key figure in Power Town. In a process that was locally described as restoration, buildings that had been officially certified as "historically significant" were remade into apartments that could be rented or sold by developers as condominiums. In this way, a "new" Turners Falls community was located in an "historic district" with buildings—such as the "Bloody Bucket Saloon"—that provide "a microcosm of Turners Falls history."[16] Advised by a Cambridge consulting firm, Urban Systems Research and Engineering, Inc., the revival was aimed at transforming Turners Falls from a "black sheep" to a "vigorous commercial and residential neighborhood."[17]

In the publicity given to these efforts, the enterprise of local and out-of-town developers was implicitly but repeatedly contrasted to the *lack* of enterprise of the population in the area that was being revived, "transient residents with no stake in the village's future."[18] At the same time, the diminished "sense of community" in the area was *blamed* on these residents, who arrived in Turners Falls with the departure of "village families" in the 1940s and '50s. By renovating old buildings, it was hoped that developers would provide the impetus for more established families to return to the area, in this way moving the "spirit" of community back, as well.[19]

The contradictions of this position were implied in discussion of the financial incentives for renovating downtown Turners Falls. Noting the potential for property owners to "reap large benefits" by renovation in a historic district, one article pointed to the tax incentives "for people who own commercial, depreciable property" and can "take 25 percent of the cost of renovations straight off their taxes the first year." Private homeowners, by contrast, would only benefit "if they converted their structures to rental properties."[20] Thus it seemed unlikely that the incentives that brought developers to Turners Falls would have the same appeal to the people who had left there 30 years previously to build homes on the hill.

The question of who was benefiting from the transformation of downstreet Turners was explicitly raised by residents who complained to the Board of Selectmen about hiring practices at Power Town. One unemployed resident protested to selectmen that "local people" could not get jobs on the project because "[t]hey're hiring out of the union hall in Chicopee."[21] Another Turners Falls resident said "We're very disappointed in the amount of local hiring. . . . There's a lot of unemployed people here who could use the work."[22] Concern was also expressed by local residents and prospective tenants that Power Town would be another tale of absentee landlords and deteriorating property. In a meeting intended to allay these concerns, the project developer tried to reassure local people that "We're not going to build it and then walk away." The newspaper noted however that the developer (now a resident of another state) was currently the absentee owner of "34 nonproject apartments downtown."[23]

Downstreet residents were also concerned about what one official described as "the $64,000 question" . . . the race of project residents."[24] In response to a woman who asked if the project was to be filled "with a lot of Puerto Ricans,"[25] project developers explained that they were required by federal rules to advertise the apartments "throughout the area, including in the Springfield newspapers."

Concern about absentee landlords and the race of project tenants underscored deep tensions surrounding the reconstruction of "community" in downtown Turners Falls by developers.[26] Widely perceived in Franklin County as a "bad" and "violent" neighborhood, residents of the area hasten to point out that it was not always this way: "It used to be beautiful—the theater, the bowling alley, the kids played ball in the evenings. But it changed . . . [it] went down. We used to have good neighbors, but they moved." A retiring Montague policeman put it somewhat differently: "It used to be, you had to talk to somebody down on the Avenue and they'd listen to you. Now they're going to talk back to you. That's their right, of course . . . but there's a very different attitude."[27]

The talk about reconstructing "community" in downtown Turners Falls evoked nostalgia for an imagined past, but ignored the contradictions and struggles that motivate its residents today. A "village" in which the paper industry is the major employer, and where a "hippie" commune[28] and absentee landlords create its image as "slum," the French and Polish-speaking congregations of Turners Falls embody a past in which ethnicity defined community. More recent arrivals lack this sense of a common past, and are known to more established residents through their common ties to state agencies such as the Department of Public Welfare and the court. For these recent arrivals in Turners, the struggle is less about "community" than about obtaining jobs and establishing themselves in run-down neighborhoods where homeless people "of no known address" roam the streets, and where social workers in Franklin County locate their most problematic clients.

A BAD NEIGHBORHOOD

One hundred and thirty (21%) of the 617 complaint applications received by the Franklin County District Court clerk between June and December 1982 were from Turners Falls, and 26 of these were

neighbor complaints from the "downstreet" area of the town. Many
involved fights between children or adults, most of which were
indistinguishable from verbal or physical exchanges recounted by
Greenfield neighbors during the same period. Complaints from
Turners were interpreted differently, however.[29] These complaints
were seen not only as a response to the fighting, but as a part of it,
and thus confirmed the view at the courthouse that fighting was the
Turners "way."

By transforming neighborhood fights and the complaints they pro-
voked into problems of self-control, the clerks were able to encourage
complainants to withdraw a charge (thereby demonstrating their
capacity for restraint) or to suggest that a complaint be "held" to "see
if there is any more trouble." While complainants typically concurred
with these recommendations, they came back days or weeks later with
variations on the same tale of violence, which over time took on the
character of a collective story about injustice and a collective demand
for the right to a life free of fighting. In one of the last hearings I
observed, which occurred at the height of local controversy over the
Power Town complex and involved an encounter between a Hispanic
woman and white ethnic complainants, one complainant spit on the
floor of the courtroom in open rebellion, flaunting her disdain for a
form of justice that she termed "a farce."

What went on in this hearing reveals the tension embodied in proceedings that are both arenas for control by the court and arenas
where the "ethics of tenacity" [the "refus(al) to accord the established
order the status of a law"][30] are practiced by complainants from the
slums of Turners Falls. It came at the culmination of several months of
fighting, in and out of court, involving 15 different complaints of
assault, of threats, and of property destruction brought to the clerk
from downstreet Turners Falls in 1982 and early 1983.[31] In the complaints, children were accused of ruining each other's clothes, setting
fires, of hitting each other, destroying each other's toys, of chasing
each other with knives, and pushing each other into buildings or trees.
In addition, adults were accused of hitting children and fighting with
each other, specifically over fences and boundaries dividing their property. At the courthouse, the hearing room was filled with people who
had been involved as either participants or witnesses to the fights. The
hearings sometimes spilled out into the hallway as the parties continued to shout and threaten each other with sticks.

In most of these complaints, the clerk transformed charges of
assault or of threats into problems of self-discipline and parental control. Parents who were behaving like children had failed to control

their children; children's fights, in turn, were defined as everyday troubles that should be "held" at the show cause level, rather than formally issued. In one of the early assault complaints in this series, a 10-year-old girl was accused of pushing another child into a tree and of threatening to "slice . . . [another's] head off." Her mother did not deny the accusation, but explained that the incident occurred because

> [the] street is a bad street. It's a violent street. Children on that street are apt to be violent. I don't know what it is. When I lived on . . . Street I didn't have these problems. Ask any Turners Falls police officer, and he'll say . . . Street is a bad street.

After hearing the accounts of the children and their mothers, the clerk said:

> Technically, I can issue it. Would you be satisfied if we issued it technically but hold it at the show cause level?[32] It's not a real vicious thing, it doesn't appear. We won't have another hearing but we'd issue it if there was more trouble. Kids push kids. [And he counseled,] One thing parents should be sure they don't do is discuss their problems in front of their kids. The kids watch TV, they want to protect the parents, they take up your fight, and first thing you know kids eight or ten or so are fighting and their fathers are slugging it out.

Here the clerk used familiar imagery—"Kids push kids"—suggesting that the root of the problem lay in the quality of parenting and thus that the complaint should not go to court. What complainants described as violence was redefined as "normal trouble," while adults were portrayed as *not* "normal," but in need of self-control. In this way, the courthouse became a forum where "common sense" assumptions about life in downstreet Turners Falls were both protested and reinforced. The mother's suggestion that the neighborhood, and not the children, were "bad," protected her child while implying that the children could be helped if the neighborhood were improved. But she also implicitly reinforced the logic used by the clerk: what went without saying for all participants in these hearings was that in "bad" neighborhoods, "vicious" behavior is not "vicious" but "normal" exchange. By issuing the complaint "technically" (and by including complainants in the decision to do so), the clerk caught them up ever more securely in the disciplines of law without making a formal charge of crime.[33] The "bad" streets that brought complainants to the courthouse remained the same, however, and complainants continued to appear at the courthouse door.

Later complaints in this series involved fights with adults and children over boundaries. The clerk also framed conflict over trespass and property damage by neighbors as "lack of self-control" by adults. For example, in cross-complaints of assault and battery by two neighbors, the conflict was defined by both sides as a problem of people who did not understand "what the right-of-way laws are," of trespass, and of property damage. For these complainants, "fighting" was a consequence of trespass. They brought official surveys to the hearing, attempting to locate the boundaries of their land. The clerk, however, said the map was "not crucial," noting that he was less concerned with right-of-way laws than with "hav[ing] this [fighting] stop." He advised everyone to "stay away from each other" and suggested that they "begin to act like adults and not children."

The complaint about right-of-way and trespass was eventually dismissed by the clerk, only to be followed 4 months later by other complaints involving the same parties, this time allied against a Hispanic woman and her four children who had recently moved to an apartment next door. In this situation, like other neighborhood disputes reaching the Franklin County court, ethnicity was not the explicit focus, yet frequently it was the subtext of complainants' stories. One complainant, a man of English ethnicity, said about the new neighbors,

> We own our own home, and when you have a house, and there's kids next door setting fires! . . . They say it's because we're prejudiced. It ain't that! If it was white kids setting fires, we'd feel the same way. . . . She complains that my kids call her kids "niggers." [But] there's one "nigger" that means "color" . . . then there's another "nigger" that means "people that lie and steal and cheat." That's the true meaning of the word! They can claim it's discrimination, because they're colored.

This complainant added that when he and his wife had first talked of moving to Turners, "people told us to watch out for the hippies . . . but we never had any problems with them. They were always polite." The real problem was "the kids," and he anticipated that "the new low-cost housing is just going to make it worse." Describing the developer of the Power Town complex as a man who "used to be a good landlord," he said that most people now felt "he fixes 'em up real fast, but when they fall apart, he doesn't do nothing."

The series of hearings involving these Turners Falls neighbors began in 1981, and suggests how the meaning of events develops over time through several linked exchanges. I focus here specifically on hearings in early 1983, in which the participants were five adults (of Polish, English, and Hispanic ethnicity) and six children. The complaints involved accusations against a child of the Hispanic woman for chasing other children with a knife; cross-complaints of assault by the adults; and a complaint by the Hispanic woman that one of the adult men threatened to "crush her face." The police described these complaints as "kidstuff," but the clerk conducted the hearings formally, asking for details of who was struck, receiving witness testimony, and attempting to restrict the range of information presented:

> Hispanic woman: How far back should I start?
> Clerk: I think we should restrict it as narrowly as possible.
> . . . If you want to start at the beginning of the day. . . .
> what precipitated the incident?

In spite of the clerk's efforts to restrict the range of testimony through repeated comments that certain information had "nothing to do with the complaint," the stories of participants aired a range of concerns about the Hispanic woman's behavior, her ways of minding her children, her job, and her children's behavior. For example, one of her neighbors stated: "She makes noise at all hours of the day. She's up and knocking around at 5:30 in the morning. . . . Who would like somebody washing clothes and taking a shower at 10:30 at night? She comes in at 2 or 3 in the morning, and she's banging and falling down." The clerk, noting that these allegations "have nothing to do with this complaint," sought to refocus the hearing by speaking to the children about what had happened: who kicked whom, where, and at what time of day. Questions directed to the adults, however, were answered in ways that expanded the discussion to trespassing by the neighbors, complaints to the police, the housing authority, and the landlord, and to the violence of "kidstuff" involving neighborhood children. One woman explained:

> [I]t all started with the knife business. . . . Earlier in the day, my son (age 6) went down to the store to get some candy. They all beat him up; he had two black eyes, and his mouth was bleeding. Then, at about 5:00, my daughter was eating with the neighbors. She had left her bike out in the alleyway, and was coming out to get it. [My son] went out to play and [the Hispanic child] went after him with a knife. My daughter came in screaming. . . . I went out, and [the Hispanic child] was coming at him. I didn't see that he actu-

ally had a knife, but [my daughter] was screaming, and [my son] was running. I brought all three kids into the house.

The clerk asked specific questions about the knife, which one complainant described as "about 5 inches long—a steak knife, with a wooden handle."[34] The mother of the Hispanic child denied that any knives had been involved, but spoke of children chasing each other with sticks.

Finally, the clerk turned off the tape recorder (a gesture that symbolically marks the end of the "formal" part of a hearing in Franklin County) and said:

> Clerk: I'm going to go off the record here. What are you folks going to do about this problem with the children?
>
> Hispanic woman: I'm moving! Because of the area, because of the people who live here!
>
> Complainant (Polish ethnicity): My children are getting abused too! It seems to be the neighborhood. Even the school says our neighborhood is bad.
>
> Hispanic woman: She doesn't control her daughter. She sticks out her tongue at us, sticks up her middle finger. . . . She calls us spics and niggers.
>
> Clerk: You know, if this goes to court, none of the peripheral issues—about noise, disturbances, disagreements—are going to be admitted into evidence.
>
> Hispanic woman: Nobody's going to do anything to just leave me alone?! We can't even go outside without them calling us spics and niggers!
>
> Complainant (English ethnicity): On the other hand, your kids call us coodies and faggots. All of the kids have a general habit of calling each other names, sticking out their tongues. As far as I'm concerned, sticks and knives is a lot worse than name-calling.

The clerk eventually took the complaints "under advisement,"[35] and the parties moved out to the hall. There, according to the Hispanic woman, one of the adults approached her saying "Just you wait!" She burst back into the courtroom, screaming to the clerk, "Can't you do something?! I can't even walk out of here!" Others alleged that she had threatened a male (Polish) complainant with a stick, and he insisted that he wanted to take out a complaint against her. The clerk attempted to calm people down, but agreed to schedule a hearing on an assault complaint for the encounter between the Hispanic woman and the Polish man in the hall.

The hearing that aired complaints about the chase with a knife and the threats to "crush" the Hispanic woman's face resulted in the issuance of two formal charges. The clerk noted that he had been dealing with these parties for over 2 years in one form or another, but that "when there's bottles and knives, and racial slurs, and the parents aren't taking any responsibility, something has to be done." He noted that the Montague police described the complaints as "kidstuff" that the parents should be able to handle, and commented that the judge might not approve of issuing formal charges. "But Chief ___, myself, and probably you, too [the anthropologist] are looking at this with a different set of values. Middle-class values, if that's what you want to call it." He recalled one complainant's comment about the neighborhood and about how the schools and police don't show any respect for the adults in the neighborhood, "and it was almost as if to say, 'If you don't issue this complaint, you're no better!'"

In the final (court) phase of this conflict (marked as final because the Hispanic woman and her children moved to another town), the assistant clerk heard the complaint brought by the Polish man alleging assault by the Hispanic woman in the hall of the court. The hearing was attended by the Polish complainant and his wife, and by the Hispanic woman. The clerk advised each side of their right to an attorney, and had the Polish complainant tell his story first:

> Complainant: Well, I guess it happened out here in the hall. We were asked to leave. She came out and gave me this scowlin' dirty look and told me, "Come on, you fat slob!" She laid down her things and said, "Come on you slob, we're goin' to have it out right here.
> Clerk: So you said she came out glarin' at you?
> Complainant: Yes—she took off her coat and put down the sticks from the [previous] hearing. . . . I started to say somethin' to her but then my wife put her hand over my mouth. She [the Hispanic woman] started up the hall with the sticks—then she put them down. I put my hands in my pockets, then she went in to Mr. Simpson [the other clerk] and said, "See, it's startin all over again."
> Clerk: So you put your hands in your pockets?
> Complainant: Yeah, I just put my hands in my pockets. I guess she was mad because she didn't get the complaint she wanted on me. She just busted right in.
> Clerk (to Hispanic woman): What would you like to say?
> Hispanic woman: I went outside and he was laughin' or mumblin'. I had the sticks in my hand. His wife held him

93

back. I came in and asked Mr. Simpson if he would escort me out because it was startin' again.

Clerk: You still livin' over there?

Hispanic woman: 'Til Friday.

Clerk: You-all still live at_____?

Polish man: Yes.

Clerk: What kind of sticks?

Hispanic woman: Sticks and stones from the other case.

Clerk: She didn't swing them at you?

Polish man: No, she threw them down.

Clerk: Were you afraid when you were out in the hall there?

Polish man: Yeah.

Clerk: What were you afraid for?

Polish man: Because my wife got me on "A & B" [assault and battery] and I just got off probation.

Clerk: You don't understand what I'm sayin'.

Polish man: I was afraid because she knows karate.

Clerk: [with a half smile and considerable skepticism] Was she in a karate stance? You weren't afraid she was going to hurt you. You were afraid you were going to violate your probation by hitting her.

Polish man: I was afraid she was going to knock the shit out of me and I couldn't hit back. She's hit me a few times in the house and I had to take it.

Clerk: You don't look like you could be pushed around.

Wife of Polish man: She made the threat when she had the sticks.

Clerk: My only concern is to have this stop. I'm sure that's what you all want.

Wife of Polish man: I want justice done.

Polish man: I want it so a female can't beat up on a guy and get away with it.

Wife of Polish man: [shouting] If I hadn't gone between those two there would have been a fight because she was furious!

Clerk: You mean you stopped *him* from fighting.

This exchange continued for some time, with the clerk probing for details that might confirm the complainant's story of threat by the Hispanic woman. Finally, he said:

It seems to me everybody's been keepin' to themselves for the last six days. It seems to me the only sensible way to end this is for everybody to keep to themselves for the next two days. Then you'll be rid of her. If I did issue this, I can tell you the judge would find her not guilty.

The wife of the Polish man became very angry at this point:

> Wife of Polish man: Threat to commit a crime is exactly what?!
> Clerk: If I hold up my fist and threaten to hit someone in the nose.
> Wife of Polish man: Then what do you think this was about?
> Clerk: I'm not goin' to argue with you about this. The two of you if you have any brains will stay away from each other.
> Wife of Polish man: [turning at the door to spit on the floor of the courtroom] This is a farce!!

In contrast to the head clerk's earlier approach to this ethnic conflict (issuing complaints so that the court could act as moral monitor), the assistant clerk denied the Polish man's application on grounds that there was no probable cause. But his exchange with the man during the hearing illuminated key issues that were implicit in this complaint, while challenging fundamental myths around which social relations are played out for some of the residents of downstreet Turners Falls. The assault charge seemed less about sticks and stones than about the threat of invasion by "outsiders" and the powerlessness of local populations to control what they experienced as invasion. Talk about powerful "spics" and weak whites ("I was afraid because she knows karate") or about strong women and weak men ("I was afraid she was going to knock the shit out of me and I couldn't hit back") spoke to this sense of powerlessness. The clerk's response, in turn, "disintegrated"[36] the imagery of the complainant, substituting his own middle class meanings for theirs: that men are more powerful than women ("You don't look like you could be pushed around") and that people who become involved in fights of this kind are brainless and irrational ("The two of you if you have any brains will stay away from each other").[37] The extent to which this hearing threw into relief the fundamental incompatibility of the life-style and values of the middle class clerk from Greenfield and those of the lower class residents of Turners Falls was evident in the fury with which the wife of the Polish complainant left the courtroom, spitting on the floor and screaming her frustration at the clerk.

COMPLAINING AS
OPPOSITIONAL PRACTICE

These hearings were simultaneously about "kids pushing kids," about developers working with federal assistance to transform a "horrendous" area into a marketable "historic district," about emergent forms of collective action by complainants and others, and about the enactment of a culture of restraint by court staff, social workers, and other local officials. The hearings monitored the "chaotic lives" of downstreet residents and constructed these lives as chaos; they both challenged and reaffirmed the order of the court by creating a space for the enactment of community ideologies within its boundaries.

For court staff, encounters such as these affirmed their own identities as rational subjects. Advising parties from Turners Falls that "if you have any brains, [you] will stay away from each other," the clerks explicitly linked rationality with avoidance, while implying that the inability to "stay away from each other" was a failure of self-control. For the clerks, these types of complaints not only told of the incapacity of Turners people for self-control, but were themselves evidence of this incapacity as narratives of chaos reenacted the conflicts and the alliances of neighborhood life in the halls and rooms of the courthouse.

For Turners Falls complainants, by contrast, complaining (to the court, as well as to numerous other state and local government agencies) was a way of *establishing* control, however transitory, in lives that were clearly *not* self-fashioned. Living in the constant shadow of these agencies, the spaces for self-assertion were constricted, dependent on relationships with others, and typically contingent on creative use of the very institutions that dominated their lives.

One woman, now in her early 20s, described a life typical of the people I spoke with. Placed in a home for "stubborn" children as a teenager when she refused to stay away from her boyfriend, she "ran" from there several times and was repeatedly brought before a judge for these acts of rebellion. When she was 17, "the judge told me I was emancipated. I didn't know what that meant." Married shortly thereafter, she gave birth to six children in 7 years, and "hasn't known what its like not to be pregnant" since she was 17. Some years after her marriage, her mother-in-law alerted the Department of Social Services (DSS) that she was having emotional problems and problems with alcohol, and could not care for her children. DSS removed the children, sending some to foster homes, others to relatives. In and out of residential facilities where her drinking and emotional problems were treated, she described herself as sometimes "a hazard to my kids"; but she consistently worked to recover them when her condition improved. Her struggle to recover also often involved negotiating with the housing authority for a larger apartment, negotiating with the treatment center to affirm her entitlement to have her children, and working with DSS to get her mother-in-law to agree that she could have her children back. Throughout this narrative of running, marriage, childbirth, institutionalization, and frequent moves, the most stable relationship this woman described was that with her social worker, who was "like a mediator" in her efforts to deal with parents, husband, mother-in-law, children, and the court.

Like the immigrant women described in Linda Gordon's (1988) study of complaints to "child-saving" agencies in the nineteenth and twentieth centuries, complainants in Turners Falls draw on available discourses (of rights, of crime, of child protection) and turn to familiar bureaucracies (the disciplinary relationships of client to social worker, of complaint applicant to clerk) to demand their right to safety and shelter. In complaint hearings, critique of the institutions, the process, and of projects such as Power Town emerges tentatively in proceedings that secure rights for people who lack "moral sense," that protect unruly children, and that provide needed governance for the "bad" neighborhoods that Power Town is intended to transform. The critique emerges out of the parodies of official court practice by defendants such as "Charlie" and from the irony with which the teenager from Turners Falls reflected on her "emancipation" hearing before the judge, as well as from the repeated appearances in court of complainants in racial conflicts, which briefly brought the clerk to "see" from their point of view. Hearings on these conflicts momentarily disrupted official readings of complaining as chaos and created a space within "kidstuff" for violence to be read as crime.

In this sense, complaining can be seen as part of what sociologist Rick Fantasia terms "emergent culture."[38] Emergent culture is always tied to the hegemonic, which "at once produces and limits its own forms of counter-culture."[39] In Turners Falls, this took shape in neighborhood fights as well as in complaints brought to the court clerk out of these fights. The fights, in turn, emerged in the context of local experiences with private developers and public officials whose hopes for creating "community" in the downstreet area involved a "facelift" but little attention to the lived experience of downstreet residents. For these residents, by contrast, coming to the courthouse to protest the "bad" and "violent" conditions in which they lived was a way of insisting on the relevance of these lives to the construction of a livable neighborhood in the downstreet area. Their complaints were often greeted with skepticism, and their allegations were sometimes the object of ridicule, but the grievances that took shape in the ongoing exchanges with the clerk defined their desire for a way of life that was *free* of fighting rather than imprisoned within it. In this sense, individual complaints brought to the courthouse became collective demands for recognition, played out over time in hearings before a clerk whose authority, in turn, depended on his capacity to "hear" and "see" what the complaints were about.

To this point in the book, my focus has been on the relationships that develop between complainants from poor or working class neighborhoods in Franklin County and the district court clerk, and on the implications of these relationships for the ways neighborhood order is shaped and collective identities defined. In the next chapter, I move away from these neighborhoods to one of the hill towns of the county, 20 miles south of Greenfield; and I move away from district court hearings to hearings before a zoning board in the town of Leverett. In a conflict that eventually was taken to superior court, neighbors in Leverett fought about the control of a hill in the middle of town, and about the meaning of the hill in the context of competing visions of property rights and of community order. The chapter points to the different meanings of going to court (as brainlessness or as virtue), depending on the class of complainants and on the forums to which they have access; and it suggests the connections of the formal power of law to the capacity of particular complainants to construct and enforce particular forms of "community" in court.

THE SINS OF PROPERTY

"We are not a bunch of eco-radicals or disgruntled neighbors. We represent a broad spectrum of folks who really care about how this town works, what makes it a great place to live in, and what it can continue to be."

Franklin County resident

The system is such that the dominant agents have a vested interest in virtue; they can accumulate political power only by paying a personal price, and not simply by redistributing their goods and money; they must have the "virtues" of their power because the only basis of their power is "virtue."

Pierre Bourdieu,
Outline of a Theory of Practice, 1977

On a warm May evening, some 30 residents of the town of Leverett in Franklin County gathered above a lake in one of the hilltowns to celebrate the end of a 4-year conflict. Carrying champagne, sparkling cider, and fresh strawberries, they arrived with their children and their dogs, greeting one another with embraces and congratulations. A fiddler under one of the stately hemlocks the group had worked so hard to save played a festive English folk tune. As dusk set in and the sky turned from orange and pink to deep gray, these successful combatants toasted their victory in converting 38 acres of forest from private property to a conservation and recreation area available to all townspeople. One of the group brought out a guitar, and in a gesture reminiscent of the 1960s spirit that animated many of those present, led them in a folksong about the struggles of the Diggers, an egalitarian movement in seventeenth-century England that attempted to "dig" (cultivate) the wastelands[1]:

In 1649 to St. George's Hill
A ragged band they called the Diggers
  came to show the people's will
They defied the landlords, they defied the laws
They were the dispossessed reclaiming what was theirs

"We come in peace" they said "to dig & sow
We come to work the lands in common
  and to make the waste ground grow
This earth divided we will make whole
So it will be a common treasury for all"[2]

The irony of these words, which captured not only the democratic ideals of the singers but the ambiguity of their position in a conflict that pitted virtuous citizens against each other, was not lost on the man who led them in the Diggers' song. Looking down over the crest of the hill at the land and comfortable houses owned by the people gathered around him, he commented wryly, "I do believe there are a few property owners among us here."

"The sin of property we do disdain
No man has any right to buy & sell the earth
  for private gain.
By theft & murder they took the land,
Now everywhere the walls spring up at their command."[3]

This chapter examines the use of law to control the moral landscape of everyday life by citizens in Franklin County whose resources (in terms of income, education, and property) were considerably greater than those of the Turners Falls residents described in Chapter 6. In the story that follows, a conflict between neighbors over a driveway becomes the focus of a lawsuit in Franklin County Superior Court and generates widespread debate about the place of property rights and of law in maintaining a local way of life. These debates point both to the central place of law in shaping a community order based on the private ownership of land, and to the ambiguous moral status of law (and especially the ideology of rights) in constructing a community understood as self-governed by equal citizens.

This is the same issue that emerged in neighbor conflicts among working class residents in Greenfield, where the assistant clerk would respond to a claim of property rights with a sermon about "limits to what is safe and legal, even on your property." Limits were defined, in part, by the rights of other property owners: for example, to safety or to quiet.[4] But there was always an implied criticism of rights talk in "little chats" by the clerk about responsibility to others and the need for self-restraint. Similarly, in Turners Falls, low-income litigants appeared at the Franklin County court with tales of trespass by new neighbors, and the clerks responded with criticism of "all these people wandering around with all these rights," and with sermons about the need for self-control.

Competing tales of law and justice unfold in these struggles. An account of boundaries and identity is presented in the vocabulary of property rights. This tale supports people's right to do what they please with their land, an idea shared by small and large property owners in a nation where property is "that which makes you what you are" and thus "that to which you have a right."[5] At a minimum, property secures the right to privacy, but it promises much more in the capacity to "build your own house"—and particularly your "dream house,"—the essence of a "self" and the ultimate definition of autonomous personhood.[6] But exercise of this right produces an alternative story about community. The story of community builds on the notion of rights but challenges the concept of autonomy to which the ideology of rights is so often linked. Rather, rights are defined as collective (the right to beauty, safety, quiet) and as dependent on the definition of common needs. The story of community may be told in a language of defiance that challenges private property as "sin" (as in the song about the Diggers), or in talk that contrasts rights to moral sense, as in the clerk's admonitions; but it may also be expressed as collective action by property owners who share common interests by virtue of land ownership in a particular area.

In the following conflict, the discourse of entitlement was mobilized and transformed by participants in a struggle that used the rights claims of individual property owners to develop a competing vision of collective interests in preserving the beauty of a local hill. Fought in town committees and in court, as well as with bulldozers and leaflets, people on different sides of the struggle evoked powerful cultural imageries of virtue and vice to explain what the conflict was about. These interpretations were shaped by the biographies of the participants, their memories of earlier struggles, and the imaginative recasting of contemporary battles as a modern reenactment of seventeenth-century egalitarianism. The capacity of parties in the Leverett conflict to hire a lawyer and file suit in superior court was central to the legitimation of these interpretations, allowing them to transform their complaint from an "interpersonal" dispute among neighbors to a matter of public policy for the town. By contrast, complaints taken to the district court clerk from Greenfield and Turners Falls were transformed *into* interpersonal matters at the court. These complaints shaped public policy only to the extent that they were viewed as a signal that fighting was out of control in certain areas, requiring official intervention to protect the safety (and the economic viability) of communities nearby.

THE LONG HILL CONFLICT

Histories

Leverett, located about 20 miles south east of Greenfield and 5 miles north of Amherst, Massachusetts, was settled in the early eighteenth century. Incorporated in 1774, it became a leading site for the manufacture of charcoal in Franklin County. Unlike Greenfield and Turners Falls, however, there is no significant industrial presence in the town today, and debates about its future focus not on industry and its demise, but on the effects of overdevelopment, as successive waves of newcomers move to the area and purchase property there for private homes. Its population has increased from 965 in 1965, just before the expansion of the University of Massachusetts in Amherst, to 1785 in 1990.[7] This increase reflects the desirability of the town as a bedroom community for university faculty, but bespeaks as well its appeal to a wide variety of others seeking an alternative to the metropolis. These include artists, craftspeople, carpenters, and builders, as well as professionals and businessmen.

Several of the key figures in the Long Hill conflict moved to Leverett as part of this influx of the 1970s and early 1980s. Politically left of center, they were in college or graduate school during the upheavals of the 1960s at Harvard, Berkeley, and Columbia, and some continued to pursue the politics of that period in their teaching and writing. Like other small towns in Franklin County, Leverett is still governed by a town meeting, which meets annually to vote on budget and policy matters. For some of these newcomers, committed to local control and to active involvement in town government, Leverett represented the possibility of community, and a move away from the individualism and materialism of modern urban life. For others, it promised the property and privacy that were increasingly scarce resources in the metropolitan centers where they grew up.

As the influx of new residents gradually spread over the landscape, transforming fields, woodlands, and houses that had stood for decades or more, the privacy and "quiet" that had drawn newcomers to the area were also transformed. Population increase and the demand for land also affected more established, often less affluent, residents of the town, as property taxes were steadily raised to support the expanded services (education, police, fire, and roads) required by the incoming population.[8]

The contest over Long Hill, a prominent landmark in the town center and the only significant hill in Leverett, emerged in the context of these pressures on land and other resources in the town. In Leverett, like the rest of the country, environmentalists had been engaged for several decades in controversy with private developers over land use. Progressively more stringent zoning by-laws were adopted by the town,[9] and in 1988 certain features of the landscape (including the Leverett Pond watershed and numerous wetlands) were designated "critical resource areas" by a vote at the annual town meeting.[10]

The central figures in the Long Hill conflict own property on or surrounding the hill and along the edge of Leverett Pond (also known as Echo Lake), which extends from the eastern base of the hill towards the town center. Most of them have long enjoyed the view provided by the hill, as well as the freedom to walk there with their children and their dogs, and some were active in efforts to designate the Leverett Pond watershed as a critical resource area. Thus the purchase of the hill in 1985, and an appeal in 1988 by the owner for a variance from the town by-laws in order to build a driveway to the summit, was viewed by homeowners at the base of the hill with alarm. While the appeal indicated that there were only plans for a single home on the summit, property owners at the base feared more extensive development.

One woman, who came originally from Pennsylvania, compared the potential development of Long Hill to environmental controversies that had engaged her parents as she was growing up. She described their opposition to a shopping center in Swarthmore, where Wanamakers, Gimbels, and "all those big Philadelphia stores moved out into this beautiful pasture." They worried about traffic problems and

> a lot of people coming out that hadn't been there before. . . . And it was again another space that was being taken up by macadam that was going to affect your community, or your environment. So I think we were really happy to move to a place that was green, and not be so close to . . . the next person. . . . That's probably why we really wanted to be here.

This woman's husband, a faculty member at the University of Massachusetts in Amherst, grew up in the New Jersey suburbs, in a "reasonably well-to-do community of New York executives." He portrayed that area, too, as one where in the 1950s "almost every lot was being taken over by development":

> So lot after lot was going, and at one point I was thinking back on just writing up a little—you know how you think you're going to write a story in your spare time? Well, my story was going to be "The Lot up the Street." It was a largish lot and there used to be grapevines there and so forth, and we [ten-year old boys] made it into a little jungle, and all of a sudden the 'dozers came in one day and just levelled it. . . .

A third participant, a lawyer active on the planning board in the nearbye town of Sunderland before moving to Leverett, spoke of a zoning ordinance there that had restricted development close to the shores of the Connecticut River, "so there could be a greenbelt. That was the thing Sunderland needed to preserve, and there was no opposition then, it passed [by a vote of] 99 to 9." Today, when people want to build near the river, "and the river is getting eaten a little bit, [the ordinance] is looked upon as a powerful thing." In Leverett, on the other hand, the thing that "needs preserving" is Long Hill: "To live in an area where there's one hill, and one hilltop, with one house on the hilltop looking down, doesn't seem to me to be a good thing to do."

Not all the opponents to development were recent arrivals in Leverett. One woman, whose husband is an insurance agent in a nearby town, described her family as "the first to pioneer here in the wintertime." She told of coming in by toboggan in the early 1950s to their property on Echo Lake, where they had purchased a lot and built a small bungalow. Eventually they were joined by others–a machinist from Greenfield Tap and Die, a station engineer for New England Power Company, a plumber, a builder, a man with a trucking business in Springfield. As soon as school ended, "we'd pack up and spend the summer here, with the boys." Today, with a plowed road, "we come up at the end of March and we won't go home until the end of November. . . . At home we live on a busy street, and if you go home and you try to sleep that first night, and oh, my . . . it's terrible. But you adjust to it, nonetheless. It's so quiet here, we just love it."

This family, whose house was built with a view toward Echo Lake, was less concerned about development ruining the beauty of the hill: "The view wouldn't make any difference as far as we were concerned." But they were worried "from the standpoint of use of the road. . . . And not only that, we've all put in deep wells, and we worried if they put up a number of houses up there, how it would affect our water system."

These concerned residents and others, most of them property owners on Long Hill Road and on Camp Road, a private way that runs along the western edge of Echo Lake, became the core of a larger group in Leverett that formed in opposition to the development of Long Hill. The core group was diverse in terms of class and income; some were permanent residents of Leverett, while others owned small summer "camps" along Camp Road and were residents of nearby cities. But they shared a concern that development of Long Hill would threaten their roads, their water, and their "quiet."

"The sin of property we do disdain . . . "[11]

Geraldine Hudson and Christopher Garfield, co-owners of a left-liberal newspaper in the Connecticut River Valley, moved to Leverett in the mid-1970s.[12] In 1985, they purchased two parcels of land on Long Hill (one of 16+ acres and one of 24+ acres). In 1987, they purchased 3 additional acres on the northwestern boundary of the 24 acre parcel [see Figure 7.1(A)] and shortly thereafter divided their entire property into four lots, two small building lots and two large lots. [Subsequently, in 1990, a third small building lot was created (lot #3 in Figure 7.1B)].

In 1988, one day before a Leverett Town Meeting that voted (94 to 5) to limit the number of rear lots that could be created from a single property or a set of contiguous properties held in common ownership,[13] and on the day after a public hearing to discuss the article that imposed this restriction, Garfield and Hudson "checkerboarded" their property. In checkerboarding, each owner conveys to the other exclusive ownership of certain portions of the land they jointly control. In this case, three of the four parcels on Long Hill (the 16 acre parcel, what had been the 24 acre parcel, and a small 1 1/2 acre parcel) were conveyed to Hudson, and one 3 acre lot was conveyed to Garfield (lot # 2 in Figure 7.1B).

Two months later, Hudson appeared before the Leverett Zoning Board of Appeals (ZBA), requesting a variance from sections III and VI of the town by-law so that she could build a house on her 16 acre Long Hill property. These sections of the by-law require that driveways serving residential premises provide access through legal frontage (200 feet of land running in a continuous line along a public way).[14] Hudson argued that the legal frontage of the 16 acre property on Long Hill Road was blocked by ledge rock and was too steep for a driveway, and

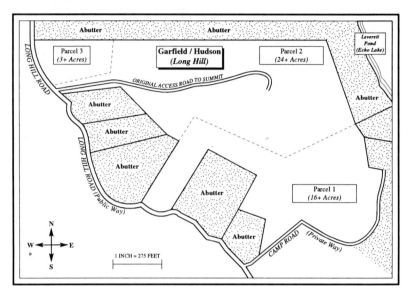

Figure 7.1A. Purchases of Garfield/Hudson, Long Hill Road, Leverett. MA, 1985 to 1987.

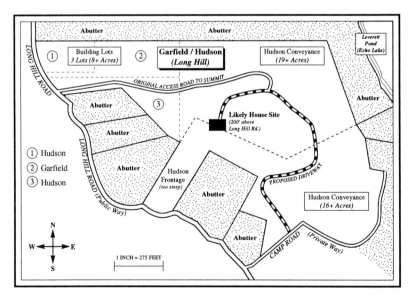

Figure 7.1B. Checkerboarding by Garfield/Hudson, Long Hill Road, Leverett. MA, 1987 to 1990.

asked for a variance that would allow construction of a driveway from Camp Road, a private way owned by the Echo Lake Association.[15] She cited a clause in the by-laws which permitted a variance if enforcement of the laws would involve "substantial hardship, financial or otherwise" to the applicant.

Hudson was represented by an attorney at the hearing, and more than fifty people, including abutters to the property, attended. While some favored the variance, many others expressed their opposition, arguing that the increased risk of runoff water down the proposed driveway might damage Camp Road, pollute Echo Lake, or contaminate shallow wells in the area. In addition they spoke of their concern about "the visual intrusion of a home at the top of Long Hill," and they submitted a petition signed by 75 residents opposing the request.

A few days after this hearing, another petition was circulated by opponents to the variance, under the title "The Long View– SaveOurScenery." Noting that "the issues here go way beyond the [owner of the hill]'s requests," the petition argued that if the variance were granted "it won't take long for others to realize that cheap back land and a variance from the ZBA add up to tremendous profits from those willing to pay top dollar for views and isolation." Focusing on what was termed "the long standing Leverett rule of 'access through frontage',", it suggested that granting the variance would set a precedent enabling the wealthy to "by-pass the by-laws."

The ZBA unanimously denied Hudson's request, noting that a variance would not be needed if she were to build the driveway through her own (or her husband's) adjoining properties (lots 1 and 2, and what subsequently became lot #3 in Figure 7.1B). The Board pointed out that these properties provided more than sufficient legal frontage, but that they were under contract to be sold, contingent on the Board's granting the requested variance.[16] Thus it suggested that Hudson's purpose in requesting the variance was simply to facilitate the most profitable use of her land, and noted with implied disapproval Hudson's use of the "hardship" clause in the town by-laws to this end. The Board concluded that "it would be unreasonable to grant relief in this case, since if it were to do so, it would have to treat other cases similarly. This would mean that the Board would have to grant a variance whenever an applicant could show . . . *that he could make more money if he didn't have to comply with the By-Law.*" The Report of the Board also pointed out that a variance in this case would "'substantially derogate'" from the intent of the bylaw "if there were adverse visual intrusion or other aesthetic impacts, or if there were adverse environmental impacts" and that "many abutters clearly felt that granting the variance might result in substantial danger of adverse visual intrusion."[17]

Hudson appealed this decision at the Franklin County court on grounds that there was new information to justify a variance,[18] and the decision was remanded back to the ZBA, which received a second petition from her in June 1989. In this petition, Hudson (who was again represented by a lawyer), repeated the earlier argument that the topography of her land made the area with legal frontage unsuitable for a driveway; she argued in addition that a failed perk test conducted on the 200 foot section that bordered Long Hill Road made it impossible to locate her house in that area, rather than on the summit. On this basis, she suggested again that a variance allowing her to build a driveway from Camp Road to the summit was warranted on grounds of financial hardship, since otherwise her lot would be rendered valueless as a building lot.

At this hearing, unlike the earlier one, the fact that Hudson and her husband owned adjacent land and that they had "checkerboarded" their property were not seen as problematic for the "hardship" argument. Focusing on the problems created by the ledge rock along Long Hill Road, and on the fact that zoning by-laws had been amended to create progressively more restrictive rules about access to residential premises through legal frontage in the period since Hudson had purchased the lot in question, the ZBA approved her appeal.[19]

Immediately after the Board's decision, a number of people who opposed the variance met on the patio of one of the modest summer "camps" along Camp Road to discuss the possibility of taking legal action against Hudson and the Zoning Board. The close connections between some members of this group and members of the Zoning Board made this a particularly awkward moment. While some of those present at the meeting (and specifically summer home owners on Camp Road) had long been outsiders in Leverett,[20] many others had been active in the town for ten or fifteen years, and had worked together with people on the Zoning Board as parents, voters, and members of other town committees. For these people, filing a suit against the Board seemed to challenge the ideology of community that had brought them to Leverett in the first place. By suing the ZBA and the owners of the hill in court, they would constitute themselves as a force *opposing* the town, in an action that many of those present interpreted as not "the Leverett way." This "way," shaped in the context of a long tradition of self-government in New England towns, is distinguished by its reliance on local procedures and the capacity for restraint that self-government implies. By contrast, going to court was interpreted as "bringing in the law" and as an unwelcome intrusion of the state in "local" matters.

This juxtaposition of state (as represented by law) and community (as represented by zoning boards, zoning by-laws, and town meetings) is reminiscent of debates in Greenfield that distinguished the *courthouse* as a symbol of local autonomy from the *court* as the locus of state law, and of struggles about autonomy and identity that took place in this building.[21] In both Greenfield and Leverett, "neighborhood problems" are seen, on the one hand, as *local* matters, to be handled by local authorities—selectmen, members of the zoning board, or the court clerk (in his guise as magistrate for "community matters). But in both places, neighbors also turn to forums that represent the power of *state* law, to enforce a specific vision of local order when they are unable to transform their desires into policy at the local level.

For poor and working class complainants in Greenfield, complaint hearings before the court clerk are such a forum, but it is typically the clerk, and not the parties before him, who constructs a particular vision of community order through these hearings. For more affluent residents of Leverett, by contrast, superior court becomes a forum where *they* construct community in court. In both settings, however, the resort to court action is viewed (sometimes by complainants, and almost always by the clerk) as morally questionable—the act of people who "can't put their hands in their pockets and walk away from conflict" (in the words of the Assistant Clerk in Greenfield). But in each, the meaning of going to court is transformed by constructions of this activity as a form of governance "by the people." In the Long Hill conflict, for example, the negative effects of court action were outweighed ultimately for those who filed suit against the Zoning Board, by a sense that it was the *duty* of opponents to keep the Board accountable by suing the town in court. For these people, "annoyed in principle that [Hudson and Garfield] seemed to have manipulated the law in such a way that they had managed to convince a small town board to go along with their view," litigation was the action of responsible citizens, who could move the conflict away from the "ridiculous level" of interpersonal hostilities by transforming it into a collective project to protect the town. Similarly, in complaint hearings before the court clerk, it became the responsibility of this official (as the representative of "community" at the courthouse) to govern greedy and irrational complainants. He did this with sermons and little chats which persuaded them to withdraw what he sometimes described as "ridiculous" complaints, by reminding them of their collective responsibilities to keep their neighborhood from becoming "like Springfield, or even New York."[22] The chief difference here is that in clerk's hearings, it was the *complainants* who became irrational and the clerk restrained; in the court hearings over Long Hill, complainants governed themselves by transforming their "ridiculous" interpersonal hostilities with greedy opponents into a civil action in superior court.

In July, 1989, just after the decision by the ZBA to grant Hudson's request for a variance, opponents filed a motion for summary judgment against the Leverett Zoning Board and Geraldine Hudson in Franklin County Superior Court. The motion asked that the variance granted by the ZBA to Geraldine Hudson be annulled, arguing that it was "detrimental to the public good" and that the Zoning Board "exceeded its authority" [under Massachusetts General Laws, chapter 40A, section 10)" by granting it.[23]

"They defied the landlords . . . "[24]

In order to obtain the political and economic support needed to carry out their legal action in court, opponents of the variance (now identified as the "Long View Alliance") engaged in a broadly based campaign to convince others in Leverett to join their cause. While several members of the Alliance had resources that enabled them to contribute generously to the suit, they could not support one on their own; in any case, a collective project required collective funding. Building on the success of earlier petitions in opposition to a variance, the group mailed a letter to Leverett residents to inform them of the suit and to solicit support of various kinds. Central to this campaign for support was the portrayal of legal action by the Alliance as a different kind of thing than recourse to law by their opponents, and specifically as more than a fight to "save the hill for themselves" by a group that was long on view, but (in the words of one resident who opposed them) "short on sight."[25]

In their letter requesting support from town residents, the Alliance explained the lawsuit as an effort to preserve a "critical resource area" from development, as well as a way of upholding "the legal and social contracts which we have forged and which bind us together."[26] By contrast, the use of law by Hudson was described as a "strategy of the wealthy." Although members of the Alliance, like their opponents, were represented by a lawyer who did not reside in Leverett, Hudson's attorneys were portrayed as people from "out-of-town" who assisted profiteers in subverting "the will of the people," undermining the rights of "the other 600 households" in town in order to secure the privileges of a few. The representation of the fight over Long Hill as evocative of the struggle for land by Diggers in 17th century England captured these alternative stories about the law, juxtaposing governance by the people ("the people's will") to the law of "the landlords," while implying that collective popular protest was a way of "reclaiming" both the land and the rights of "the people."[27] By likening their own use of law to the defiance of the landless, the Alliance transformed their own "sins of property" (after all, they, too, were landowners, and were using the law of trespass to argue their case in court) into the virtues of a collective struggle for common land.

Not all residents of Leverett were convinced by this representation of the Alliance as pursuing town interests and of Hudson and and her husband as wealthy profiteers. For example, one supporter of the ZBA decision noted the relative affluence of many of the central figures in the opposition, the proximity of the hill to their own back yards, and the threat posed to their way of life by an increasing number of even more affluent professionals who had recently moved into the area and were rapidly buying up land. A second supporter of the variance suggested that opponents were simply attempting to keep people from moving to Leverett: "They have their piece of the pie, so why can't they let others have a piece as well?" Even those who opposed the variance expressed discomfort with a position that was environmentally sound but that seemed at the same time to be "shutting the barnyard door" in Leverett. In this light, *opponents* became "greedy," and their suit suggested that the law was being used to secure as large a piece of the pie as possible for themselves. As one local builder pointed out some months later, "Do you know what having a conservation area behind your property does to its value?"

While some members of the Alliance acknowledged the contradictions in their position, they saw their work in developing the lawsuit as a way of transforming what one member of the group described as "a private property system that by and large keeps people apart" into "something dynamic that cross-cut boundaries. If it weren't for the technicalities of the legal system and the need for money, we wouldn't have been forced to act collectively. But if we didn't develop a large group, we couldn't pursue the case."

Aided by a supportive real estate lawyer who owned property at the base of the hill and by the efforts of one woman who had previously carried out legal research, the group identified numerous legal precedents to support their claim that a variance was inappropriate, and that none of the conditions required for granting one had been met in this case.[28] Working with a sympathetic Greenfield attorney who helped them sort out the issues that would and would not work in court, they discovered that in spite of what one of the group described as "lawyers' technicalities," they were able to develop an argument to which "the judge listened and paid attention."

Just as these collaborative efforts seemed to affirm their sense that it was possible to use the legal system creatively for collective, rather than simply private, ends, the exchanges between members of the Alliance and the owner of the hill escalated into increasingly hostile encounters. Angered by the continued logging of the hill while the suit was pending, members of the Alliance sought to block access to it in various ways. They erected "No Trespassing" signs at the entrance to Camp Road, requested a "Stop Work" order from the Franklin County Building Inspector, and filed a complaint with the police. When none of these efforts was successful, the Alliance appealed to the town Select Board, arguing that because court action was pending, the owners had no right to proceed with their development of the hill (that is, with the logging). The Board referred the matter to the Town Counsel, who argued that the town had no jurisdiction in this matter because the trespass involved Camp Road (a private way). This was therefore a private quarrel, and not a matter of public (town) concern.

The most imaginative of the Alliance's efforts to prevent access to the hill was what they termed the "Memorial Day Reforestation Project." On May 30, 1990, members of the group planted several small pine trees across the road being used to log the hill, at its intersection with Camp Road, in a symbolic gesture to prevent tractors and other heavy equipment from getting through (see Figure 7.2). The man who was doing the logging "ran his tractor around the trees," but the owners of the hill came "in a silver Saab" and "ripped up all the trees." After this, "a bunch of people went with post-hole diggers and posts, eight of these," and placed them across the road with logs between them and a sign forbidding movement across the barrier (see Figure 7.2). The posts were also removed by the owners of the hill; but these actions by both sides evoked precisely what one member of the Alliance had earlier described as the "ridiculous level" of interpersonal hostilities that they sought to avoid by going to court, setting in question the fragile boundary between responsible action by "respectable citizens" (as symbolized by the legal suit) and the angry response of disgruntled neighbors or "eco-radicals." Indeed, the "Memorial Day Reforestation Project" is reminiscent of the "spite fence," a familiar strategy in neighbor conflicts both in Greenfield and elsewhere in the United States.[29]

Figure 7.2A. "Memorial Day Reforestation Project"

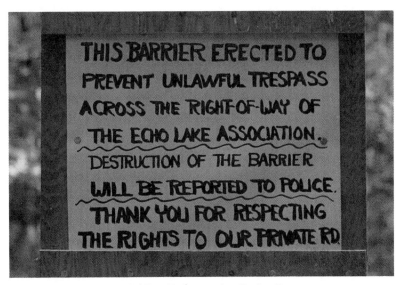

Figure 7.2B. "Memorial Day Reforestation Project"

Figure 7.3. The Long Hill "Theme Park"

The Alliance continued during these months to appeal to the town for support, handing out leaflets at the town dump (where many residents appeared regularly on Saturdays and Sundays) and sending a renewed appeal through the mail. In a letter that began with the words "URGENT—PLEASE HELP US TO SAVE LONG HILL—URGENT" they outlined the issues as they saw them, the steps that they had taken to prevent development of the hill, and the legal grounds for their opposition to the variance.

In September, members of the Echo Lake Association invited town residents to a picnic and get-together at the Leverett Pond, with a flyer that depicted Long Hill as a "theme park" with a special exit along the state highway (see Figure 7.3). Like the the song about seventeenth century Diggers, and the "Memorial Day Reforestation Project," this representation of Long Hill as theme park blurred the boundaries between the battles of disgruntled neighbors, on the one hand, and the moral struggles (historical and contemporary) between those who would "work the lands in common" and those who would "buy and sell the earth for private gain," on the other.[30]

"This earth divided we will make whole . . ."[31]

On the 29th of October, 1990, the Franklin County Superior Court granted the request by members of the Alliance for a summary judgment against the Leverett Zoning Board and Geraldine Hudson. This judgment reversed the decision of the Board to grant a variance that would allow Hudson to construct a driveway from a private way (Camp Road), rather than through legal frontage on Long Hill Road (figure 7.1B), and remanded the case to the Zoning Board for reconsideration.[32] In reversing the Board's decision, the court order legitimized the Alliance's interpretation of why a variance was inappropriate, and endorsed their claim that granting it would constitute a trespass on the Camp Road property of the Echo Lake Association. Thus while the court order affirmed their vision of how community rules should be applied in Leverett, and consolidated the position of the Alliance as keeper of these rules, it did so by reaffirming a system of property rules that, as one of the parties to the suit noted "is stacked in favor of the wealthy." This man added, "We assumed it was stacked against us; yet common sense worked, in spite of the lawyers' technicalities." The sense that the victory in court was not simply a victory for the wealthy was emphasized in local news reports, as well, which described the project as involving the adoption of zoning regulations to "restrict building on hillsides and mountaintops for aesthetic reasons"[33] and as a way of "show[ing] . . . other people that efforts to change something on the grass-roots level can pay off."[34]

An appeal of the court's decision by Hudson was unsuccessful, and in February 1991 the Leverett Zoning Board formally reversed their 1989 decision and denied the variance they had granted over a year and a half earlier. Immediately after this, Hudson's lawyer approached the Alliance with a tentative offer to sell the hill, and an extensive campaign was begun in Leverett to raise the money needed for the purchase. In addition, negotiations were begun with the Valley Land Fund, a not-for-profit voluntary organization, to act as purchaser on behalf of the Alliance, and a commitment of funds was obtained from the Rattlesnake Gutter Trust, a local conservation land trust. Several members of the Alliance also drew on trust funds to contribute to the purchase price. Finally, negotiations with Hudson led to an agreement that she would contribute a taxdeductible donation of 35% of the price of the land.

A real estate lawyer who was actively involved in the purchase described its final stages:

> We were 30 [thousand] shy, and that's when we put leaflets in mailboxes, and Camp Road came in with, everybody contributed the max that they could . . . and it just brought all the entire town together. A number of neighbors, including some new arrivals, said "We just don't have the cash in hand right now, but we'll give you, you know, $500 a year for the next. . . ." One person gave us $50 a month for the next two years because that's all he could afford, because he thought, he didn't even live here yet, he'd bought a piece of land to build a house in the future. . . . And it was exciting because to me this thing that started with lawsuits and divisions, especially with the town being divided, all got together for this common end to preserve a hill, save a backdrop to the town lake, the thing that you see on the second floor of town hall when you go there.

The campaign to raise money coincided with favorable publicity about the impending purchase in several local papers.[35] One article described the purchase as a "unique form of conflict resolution" in which residents of the town wanted to "buy a strategic piece of land to prevent it from being developed and spoiling their view." The article noted that the purchase would "end several years of feuding between the land's owner and a group of neighbors," and focused on the role of the Valley Land Fund as an intermediary in converting the land from private property into an area for passive recreation and conservation.[36]

On the 15th of May 1991, the Valley Land Fund, acting as agents for the Long View Alliance, bought the land on Long Hill from Geraldine Hudson. More than 70 of the approximately 600 families in town had contributed to the costs of the lawsuit and the purchase, in amounts ranging from $25 on up to several thousand. On the following day, residents from Long Hill and Camp Roads and their supporters gathered on top of the hill in the celebration that was described at the beginning of this chapter. The mood of the gathering was indeed jubilant. The Alliance had succeeded in the suit and in the purchase, but equally important was their capacity to do it without having people "split off and go their separate ways." Instead, "when one got burnt out, others took it up," so that as a group, in the words of the man who led the gathering in the Diggers' song, "we were able to sustain [an] incredible commitment of time and energy from ourselves and dozens of other people over a very long period of time, without any particular reward other than the evolving friendships and good feelings within our various groups."

The long legal and political struggle to "save the hill" was won by acquiring it; but this affirmation of the "common sense" that the best way to control neighboring land is to buy out the owner was transformed by a strategy of participation that cut across conventional divisions of class, of wealth, and of occupation in Leverett and sketched a concept of entitlement (and of "need") as collective rather than as simply a matter of private "rights." This transformation from private right to collective need was made possible by the complex politics involved in the purchase of the land, and its subsequent donation to a local conservation trust that would administer it as a recreation area for the public.

Gifts are, as Bourdieu has noted, "intrinsically equivocal, ambiguous conduct."[37] Like other forms of debt relation, gifts "have . . . the power of founding either dependence or solidarity, depending on the strategies within which they are deployed."[38] The donation of the hill to the town for recreation and conservation placed the transaction "under the veil of enchanted relationships,"[39] that is, as an operation for and about collective entitlements and needs. Indeed, participation by the previous owner of the hill as a "giver" (through a tax writeoff provision) was one dimension of this enchantment, quite explicitly directed at healing divisions that were widened or created in the long conflict and at suggesting consensus about the meaning of the hill for the town. Another dimension was the arrangement made by the Long View Alliance with the Valley Land Trust to act as its agent in purchasing the hill. This arrangement helped to secure the status of the land as "common" good rather than as the privilege of a few.

The gift to the land trust not only established the hill as common land, however but it established the power of specific givers to define how the town by-laws would be enforced, whose view would be enhanced, and who could use the law to establish control over Leverett's future. In this way the Long View Alliance temporarily displaced neighbors who threatened their self-interests, intruding on their view and "degrading" their properties, while establishing their own capacity to authorize and legitimate a particular interpretation of "common" good. It also connected a number of individuals and groups in carrying out a collective project, however, and this process seemed to gain continued momentum after the purchase of the land was complete.[40]

The law was a key tool in this construction of a particular vision of community in Leverett by the Long View Alliance. The notion that going to court was not the "Leverett way" suggested a vision of community outside the law, just as the notion that the Long Hill project was like the struggles of landless Diggers suggested a vision of protest that defied law. Like the story of the Diggers, the story of Long Hill is a tale about removing a piece of land from private to common ownership. It is also a tale about evolving friendships and collective work that "cross-cut boundaries." Unlike the Diggers, however, the Long Hill project was shaped within a law that structured not only the town by-laws on which members of the Alliance drew to argue their case in court, but which permitted them, as owners of property at the base of Long Hill, to frame their suit in superior court in the language of trespass. By contrast, the "other half of America" must rely on "community" hearings, where their "ridiculous" interpersonal problems may occasionally be interpreted as serious matters of public concern by the court clerk.

CHAPTER 8

PLAYING WITH RIGHTS

"The law is the instrument of official power; in this sense it is central as nothing else is."

James Boyd White,
Justice as Translation, 1990

This book has described some of the ways that local courts are used to construct neighborhood order by citizens and by court officials in two Massachusetts counties. A key theme of the book is that in spite of the ideology of restraint, of law avoidance, and of self-help that is documented in much of the ethnographic literature about law and court use in the United States,[1] the law is "central as nothing else is" among the people who were the focus of this study, whether or not they actually appeared at the courthouse with a complaint. As Chapter 7 suggests, the law is as important to a "local" way of life that is distinguished by its *separation* from state law, as it is to a way of life in which fights between family and neighbors at the courthouse are routine. State law infuses town by-laws, zoning board hearings, and town meetings, shaping impassioned speeches by environmentalists about the rights of herons and jack-in-the pulpits,[2] as well as talk about the way responsible citizens—"nice, respectable, people"—can keep town boards accountable by suing them in court.

In bringing such suits, complainants who viewed the technicality and expense of a lawsuit as features that set the legal system apart and "stacked [it] in favor of the wealthy," discovered that their "common sense" and that of the superior court judge were the same. This shared common sense, in which the boundaries of private property became a framework for the interpretation of rights and transgressions, allowed the plaintiffs in the Long Hill conflict to affirm their position as keepers of community values. In mobilizing the law, these complainants affirmed their right to *be* self-governing citizens in a society where "property" and "propriety" are "interchangeable terms,"[3] and in which the ideal of the citizen, "virtuous in his devotion to the public good," but virtuous too in his autonomy as a landowner, has deep roots.[4]

In Greenfield and Turners Falls, by contrast, complainants who *knew* the law was "stacked against them," and whose "common sense" was typically contested in hearings before the court clerk, were engaged in little chats that encouraged them to "choose" dismissal or agree to a "technical issuance," as a way of showing their capacity for restraint. In hearings that were reserved for the "relational troubles" of the working class and welfare poor, parties were embedded ever more securely in a system of justice that assigns the governance of "garbage cases" and "garbage people" to the lower court, and engages court staff in perpetual conversation with the poor and propertyless. In more elite forums, by contrast, legal professionals engage a more privileged audience, and make worlds (in superior court decisions, in the legal academy, and so forth) that are "shaped by reason" so as to secure the rights (and the virtuous personhood) of civilized men.[5]

Thus, complaining is productive of hierarchies that distinguish upper from lower courts, property from personal conflicts, and wealthy from low-income complainants. Poor complainants who turn to the court to resist the class and gender bias of the families and neighborhoods in which they live are guaranteed the right to be heard, but little else, while more affluent complainants affirm their rights to property and community in court.

As this discussion suggests, the pervasiveness of what Tocqueville described as "the spirit of law" and its capacity to "enwrap the whole of society," is a dimension of its place in constituting hierarchies and relationships that are at the heart of the social fabric, so that it catches people up in ways that are "hardly noticed."[6] This process of being "caught up" in the law is complex, however. It is subjecting, in the sense that both affluent and poor complainants frame their wants and their needs in terms that tend to confine them to pre-existing relations, traditions, and institutions as they go to court, speak with a lawyer, appear before a zoning board, call the police, talk to a social worker, or fight with their neighbor. These relations and traditions are what constitute the "disciplines and demands"[7] of the power of law.

At the same time, these disciplines are effective as "disciplines," working "as a mode of action upon actions,"[8] because of the multiple ways in which people "lastingly 'bind' each other"[9] as clerk and complainant, or as neighboring property owners. These relations involve competing, often contradictory, demands. The overlapping meanings of "private" complaints as an expression of the court's "community" function, as the "brainless" cases of irrational people, and as potential signals of serious crime, produce the complex dynamics of complaint hearings that are at the same time a space for subjection and for opposition, and that catch up not only the parties to complaints but court staff in what Raymond Williams has termed a "moving hegemony."[10] The concept of a "moving hegemony" allows for the coexistence of discipline and struggle, of subjection and subversion, and directs attention towards a dynamic analysis of what it means to be caught up in power. In this analysis, the invention or subversion of culture (or of law) emerges as part of the active process of hegemony, and in the "always differing performances" of culture.[11] Thus, for example, complaint hearings in Franklin County are sites for the surveillance of poor populations and "undesirable" people in Turners Falls, but they also become a space for maneuver for these complainants and defendants, as they discover rights and crime in the "garbage cases" that are excluded from more elite arenas. This use of the law depends, however, on their relationship with an official who can sometimes "see" from their point of view, as well as on their capacity to be persuaded to "see" from his.[12]

The contrast of complaint practices in Franklin County and in Essex (discussed in Chapter 5) is illuminating here. In Franklin County, where dismissal rates in complaint hearings were identical to those in Essex, and where complaints brought to the clerk were also described as "garbage," the meaning of garbage cases and of clerk's hearings was tied to a regional history in which the courthouse was a symbol of resistance against state power. Court staff in Franklin County were part of this history, just as they were caught up in the ideology of law as a system of rules and a form of reasoning that separate legal institutions and legal professionals from the everyday settings and relationships that bring people to court. "Garbage cases" both marked this boundary and continually transgressed it in a region where the identity of the courthouse as a symbol of county government depended on the *connections* between legal space and local space. Garbage cases were to be "weeded out," but they also demanded "keying in." This transformed the courthouse into an institution that could share the surveillance of "the other half of America" with the social workers whose clients appeared there so regularly;[13] but it also created a space for hearing the "little problems" of people with more familiar lifeways, whose demands for a livable neighborhood were sometimes heard by the court clerk.

At the Essex court, by contrast, the contradictions that were at the heart of complaining in Franklin County were disentangled administratively by the compartmentalization of complaints into interpersonal quarrels (suitable for mediation), criminal problems (appropriate for the court proper), and routine administration (bad checks, welfare fraud, suitable for administrative processing by the clerk). The identity of this court as a *legal* institution depended on these distinctions between legal and everyday space and legal and everyday knowledge, and on the differences between professional and lay magistracy, distinctions that have marked the professionalization of law from the mid-eighteenth century onward. The official division of labor in Essex between mediation, administration, and law transformed the meaning of clerk's hearings at this court into a space for the routine. This, in turn, affected the practice of the clerk (not only in debt cases, but in the decreasing numbers of neighbor and family cases he handled). The colloquial language of harassment, "yeling" and "stairing" in which complaints were filed (with the tacit permission, but without the involvement of the clerks) led to hearings focused on the differences between harassment or "yeling" and real crime. This both reconfirmed the divisions of a juridical field where "real law" was practiced upstairs, and constrained the clerk's capacity for surveillance, as well as his space for maneuver in using the law.

In Franklin County, by contrast, the court could serve as an arena for local governance only if it was perceived as responsive to local needs, and needs were both discovered and invented in talk about noisy motorcycles, smashed pumpkins, fighting children, and girdled trees. The translation of what were often described as "ridiculous" complaints into the official language of law was at the heart of this process of invention, and involved both clerk and complainants in hearings that were not simply about a way of life in which everyone fights. In an area where the right to be let alone was not only an issue for residents with new neighbors, or for homeowners worried about a new apartment complex, but for court staff in an institution increasingly dominated by its identity as part of a state system of justice, conflicts about privacy and autonomy were deeply resonant for all participants and produced the intense exchanges that so often transformed complaint hearings into condensed reenactments of family tensions or of neighborhood politics.

In this sense, Franklin County hearings were collaborative processes in which the clerk's power as translator depended on the engagement of complainants, an engagement that was secured by the "fiction"—one constructed jointly by the clerk and the parties, but made possible by the historical position of the court in this area—that the hearings *were* legal events. This permitted the movement between law and morality that characterized the practice of the Assistant Clerk; and it meant that both garbage and the law could occasionally be resignified in the exchanges of the clerks with the parties to complaints.

This process of resignification was not always done in the language of claims, as the analyses in Chapter 6 suggest. Rather, it involved practices that altered spaces[14] by momentarily reconstituting the court through the physical presence and the point of view of people from downstreet Turners Falls. Charlie made a mockery of law as much in his dress as in his style of argument, but he was able to do so because he had a receptive audience in a court staff whose view of the law as a "wet noodle" was confirmed in his performance (and through their self-mocking response to his performance). Similarly, the Assistant Clerk was also able to reinvent the law in terms of familiar cultural figures that he located in the changing neighborhoods of Greenfield and nearby towns: "disturbing the peace" was at the same time a businessman "trying to make a go of it" in a transitional neighborhood that "used to be quiet"; "assault" was reinterpreted as a parent whose failure to control his tongue leads the children to take up his fight out on the street, as a "macho man" whose lack of restraint brings the ghetto to Turners Falls, or as a "pushing match in which someone threw the first punch" outside a local bar. In this way he was able to persuade complainants to see from his point of view and produced the double reality of decisions that were both imposed and chosen.[15] But this was only possible because the clerk was able to see from *their* point of view, as well. He failed at this sometimes,[16] producing a law that made no common sense, and instigating the rebellion of complainants who spit on the floor of the courthouse in defiance.

Complaint hearings at this court thus became *"a way of using imposed systems,"*[17] even as they further enmeshed participants in a legal order which "infiltrates through society right down to the lowest ranks."[18] In the exchanges of court staff with the subjects of garbage cases, the courthouse became a site for the production of a complex local culture of opposition to law, shaped at the intersection of many diverse oppositions. This oppositional culture was not a coherent stance, just as the resistances I have described are often tentative and emerge only in particular relational contexts. Nonetheless they are collaboratively shaped, although in very different ways, by court staff, by complainants, and by those they accuse.

While complaint hearings transformed the court into a space for maneuver for staff and for the least affluent citizens in Franklin County, the superior court was drawn into the struggles of wealthier property owners. More elite cases are also revealing of the complex ways in which oppositional practices are tied to hegemonic ones, as the 11 plaintiffs in the Long Hill conflict used their rights to privacy as property owners in order to transform a neighbor's hill into common ground. This enhanced the value of their own land; but it also shaped a collective project that (in their own experience) cross-cut the conventional boundaries dividing people in the town of Leverett. The project also created new divisions, however, and in order to mobilize broader community support, the group engaged in an intensive campaign about the potential of Long Hill as a conservation and recreation area for the town.

This campaign involved the Alliance in a playful appropriation of imageries from other struggles engaged in by less established resistors, including those of landless Diggers in seventeenth century England and of environmentalists involved in reforestation projects. Their "Reforestation Project" on Memorial Day superimposed the meanings of efforts to combat the World Bank and other forces of destructive development in the Third World onto their barricade of a "logging road" that threatened the trees on Long Hill; and their organization of a community picnic on invitations that represented Long Hill as a "theme park" evoked familiar cultural stereotypes of tacky development driven by greedy outsiders. In other literature, their opponents were portrayed as "profiteers" bringing a "Trojan Horse" for uncontrolled development to the town, in this way threatening the control of "regular taxpayers" like themselves over the government and future of Leverett. These constructions were self-consciously ironic in a group that sought to dispel notions that it was dominated by "eco-radicals," but that included people who were committed to using the law to construct a more collective interpretation of entitlement than that implied by privacy rights. While their public campaign for support was not persuasive for some, they were able to collect sufficient pledges to finance both a lawsuit and the eventual purchase of Long Hill. In doing so, they reaffirmed the central place of property rights in the moral landscape of the town and improved their position as property owners, but transformed Long Hill (and the rights that protected it) into a collective space, much as complainants before the clerk reaffirmed the status of their troubles as "personal" and relational, even as they made "community" trouble at the court.

Clearly there is a difference between the Long View Alliance and complainants who appeared before the court clerk, even the most affluent of these. The Alliance could fight about a way of life in the discourse of property rights because they controlled property and other resources, and their particular histories and education made them skilled interpreters of the local and translocal meanings of Long Hill as private land and collective entitlement. By contrast, working class and low-income complainants in show cause hearings were restricted to the language of crime, to their capacity to occupy the courtroom, and to their dependence on a clerk who could interpret violence as more than a way of life, and complaints as more than garbage. Nonetheless, in both contexts the engagement of these actors with the court and with other local agencies both enmeshed them in the law and gave them a position from which to speak.

This analysis suggests the limitations of an interpretation that sees subversion or "small resistances" principally as a diagnostic of "overlapping and intersecting forms of subjection."[19] The resistances described in this book are surely a diagnostic of power, but they are also about the "tricks" and the "tenacity" in which the established order is refused its meaning as law.[20] These forms of play with the law emerge within a relationship of power, and are enacted through and in opposition to it.[21] Thus, complaining, like the forms of resistance documented in a number of other works, consists in "a complex admixture of tacit (even uncomprehending) accommodation to the hegemonic order at one level and diverse expressions of symbolic and practical resistance at another" which are themselves productive of power.[22]

In a recent interview, Jamaica Kincaid was asked about an experience she described in her latest book, *Lucy*, where the heroine tells of being forced to memorize Wordsworth's "I wandered lonely as a cloud" as a child growing up in a colonial school. Kincaid explained:

> Every colonial child has to do that. It's a two-edged thing because I wouldn't have known how to write and how to think if I hadn't read those things. I wouldn't have known my idea of justice if I hadn't read *Paradise Lost*, if I hadn't been given parts of *Paradise Lost* to memorize. It was given to me because I was supposed to be Satan. The last chapter of the book that I have written has a lot of things about that. The book is called *Lucy*, short for Lucifer.[23]

This passage points to the complicated interplay of subjection and creativity in relations of power, and of how oppression at one moment in time becomes part of the self, providing a basis for resistance in the future. Lucy describes her childhood vow "to erase from my mind, line by line, every word" of Wordsworth's poem,[24] yet Kincaid's memory of this experience becomes the autobiographical context for her West Indian *au pair* narrator's struggle with a white, middle class employer to whom she is both bound and refuses to submit; similarly, by constructing the central character in *Lucy* around her own childhood enactment of Satan in *Paradise Lost*, Kincaid remakes her subjection in the colonial relationships of her childhood into "a different thing, something new."[25]

Some years ago, in a discussion of a suit by the Mashpee Wampanoag Tribal Council in federal court for possession of 16,000 acres of land in Mashpee, Cape Cod's "Indian Town," James Clifford suggested that identity be conceived "not as a boundary to be maintained but as a nexus of relations and transactions actively engaging a subject."[26] Clifford argues that while the legal claim required the Mashpee to prove their identity as a tribe, the trial "seemed to reveal people who were sometimes separate and 'Indian,' sometimes assimilated and 'American.' Their history was a series of cultural and political transactions, not all-or-nothing conversions or resistances."[27] Indeed, the suit itself was part of a process of reinventing tribalism, "a reinterpretation of Mashpee's contested history in order to act—with other Indian groups—powerfully, in an impure present-becoming future."[28]

Like Kinkaid's description of the invention of Lucy from her own embodiment of Lucifer in the colonial relationships of her childhood, Clifford's analysis of the Mashpee trial has been helpful to my thinking about the connection of invention to tradition, and of subjection to subversion. His notion of identity as a nexus of relations helps to reinfuse "structures" of authority with subjects who both embody and can transform them, who "lastingly bind each other,"[29] but whose use of oppressive relations may also reinvent them.

The potential for creativity in this process is located in what Winnicott calls the "continuity-contiguity moment,"[30] that is, in the blurring of Lucifer/Lucy, of me/not me, of garbage cases and court cases, or of autonomy and engagement. This blurring allows for movement beyond familiar forms, but the "beyond" is also always already there, discovered or "found" in the familiar like "the simple unearthing, at once accidental and irresistible, of a buried possibility."[31] In the Long Hill conflict, the creative appropriation of cultural imageries of resistance blurred the boundaries of a fight that defended private property, on the one hand, and fights *against* private property, on the other, merging eco-radicals with virtuous citizens in a battle that was both about common ground and about protecting specific back yards. At the courthouse, Charlie's antics appropriated familiar defense practices, merging his local identity as street person with the rational persona of a lawyer, in this way "inventing" his right to shelter at the county jail, while transforming the law into a "wet noodle." And in complaint hearings, a clerk who was part magistrate, part beat policeman, transformed hearings into "little chats," making the court into a forum for morality, but sometimes participating in the conversion of morality into collective rights.

The "double reality" of these processes is that they are both about domination and about refusal, about complicity with power and struggles against relations of power, and that neither of these processes is a "mask" for the other. This double reality provides the space for maneuver in hearings that interrogate the court, rupturing legal knowledge "from the perspective of what it expels [garbage, lay knowledge]";[32] but it also produces clerks as "watchdogs," and transforms complainants into "the other half of America," people whose subordinate position is manifest in their repeated efforts to govern the conditions in which they live.

NOTES

Notes to Preface

1. Carolyn Steedman, in her account of a working class childhood, describes the lives of her subjects as "lived out on the borderlands" (Steedman, 1986, p. 5).

Notes to Acknowledgements

1. *Legal Studies Forum*, 1985.
2. See Mahoney and Yngvesson, 1992.
3. See Greenhouse, Yngvesson, and Engel, 1993.

Notes to Chapter I

1. New York Times, May 19, 1991, p. 14.
2. Mather and Yngvesson, 1980-81; Yngvesson and Mather, 1983.
3. Yngvesson, 1976.
4. Danzig, 1973; Danzig and Lowy, 1975; McBarnet, 1981; Ryan, 1981; Abel, 1982; Harrington, 1985.
5. *Massachusetts General Laws*, chapter 218(35A):55; Administrative Office of the District Court Department, *Standards of Judicial Practice*, 1975, 3:00.
6. In both Salem and in Franklin County, a research assistant (Randy Silnutzer) worked with me in observing hearings and conducting interviews.
7. Parties to complaints were interviewed selectively. In some cases, particularly the most complicated neighborhood conflicts, we attempted to speak to all of the principals as well as to others who were less immediately involved, but familiar with the events and the parties. These interviews typically lasted between 1 and 3 hours, and covered not only the conflict, but a range of social, economic, and political issues that participants viewed as relevant to the interpretation of the conflict. In other cases, participants were interviewed briefly before or after a complaint hearing to learn about their familiarity with the court, their reasons for bringing the complaint to the clerk, their relationship with other parties, and a brief history of the conflict. In many cases, particularly as complaints began falling into familiar patterns, we relied solely on the application form and the hearing itself for information about a conflict. Names and identifying information about parties have been changed.
8. A number of works take up this issue, focusing on the interpretation of court use as evidence of greed, lack of self-control, and dependence (see,

e.g., Engel, 1984; Greenhouse, 1986; and Merry, 1990; for a more general discussion of the meanings of law in American culture, see Greenhouse, Yngvesson, and Engel, 1993).

9. Stone, 1988, p. 7. Stone is discussing what she terms "the essence of policy making in political communities." See also Mather and Yngvesson, 1980–1981, pp. 776–782; Greenhouse, 1982, p. 70; and Yngvesson, 1988a, pp. 116–119 for a discussion of disputing as the negotiation of order.

10. See, generally, Foucault, 1982. Mitchell, 1990, p. 574, building on Foucault's work, describes power as "creating truths and subjects and sites of apparent autonomy." And see Abu-Lughod, 1990, p. 50.

11. Abu-Lughod, 1990, p. 41. The concept of trouble as "crystallizing" is drawn from Emerson and Messinger, 1977, p. 127, who describe how "in moving through a circuit of troubleshooters, an initially ambiguous trouble tends to crystallize, as new means of dealing with the problem are sought out and impelemented and prior ways are determined to be ineffective and rejected."

12. Hoebel, 1954, pp. 29–45. Emerson and Messinger, 1977, p. 131, argue that "trouble comprehends and incorporates both the openness and indeterminacy of deviant outcomes, in part by abandoning the centrality of the notion of deviance itself."

13. Abu-Lughod's (1990) article, "The Romance of Resistance: Tracing Transformations of Power Through Bedouin Women," emphasizes this point. See, in particular, Abu-Lughod 1990, p. 50.

14. Ibid., p. 42.

15. Gordon, 1988.

16. Ibid., p. 294.

17. Ibid., 1988, p. 258.

18. Ibid., pp. 298 and 371 (footnote 5).

19. Ibid., p. 281.

20. Bourdieu, 1977, p. 5. Bourdieu argues that two opposing truths coexist in social practices, the "so-called objective truth" of the observer and the subjective experience of an exchange. He suggests that the meaning of social practices derives from the response they trigger, "even if the response is a failure to reply that retrospectively removes its intended meaning." In this case, the opposing truths of local trouble include complainants' claims that it is crime and official definitions of local trouble in certain neighborhoods as "nothing real vicious" that should be handled by partici pants themselves.

21. See Bourdieu's discussion of the way "relations of domination are made, unmade, and remade in and by the interactions between persons," and of the processes through which "agents lastingly 'bind' each other" in these relations (Bourdieu, 1977, pp. 184, 196). Clearly, I disagree with Bourdieu's assumption that this is only a phenomenon of nonstate societies. See also Greenhouse (1991, p. 34, and especially footnote 14 on p. 60), who notes (quoting Bourdieu, 1977, p. 183) that "it appears that everywhere, 'relations of domination can be set up and maintained only at the cost of strategies which must be endlessly renewed,' and that such contests take place in a wide variety of forms and contexts."

The interpretation of meanings as emerging in relational engagement is elaborated theoretically in Bakhtin's discussion of meaning as occurring *between* self and other, and of utterance as "always an answer" (Holquist,

1990, p. 60), as "a border phenomenon. . . . [which] takes place between speakers" (Holquist, 1990, p. 61). At the same time, action and response are always shaped by dominant discourses "whose content is always already performable by the general members of the population" (Terdiman, 1985, p. 62; and see Holquist, 1990, p. 145). For a theoretical account of subjectivity that locates the capacity for "inventing" meanings in relations of inequality and domination, see Mahoney and Yngvesson, 1992.

22. Moore, 1972, p. 77; Mather and Yngvesson, 1980-1981; Comaroff and Roberts, 1981, p. 29. For earlier work that pointed in this direction, see Colson, 1953 and Turner, 1957.

23. Comaroff and Roberts, 1981, p. 19.

24. Nader, 1965, 1969; Nader and Todd, 1978. This move was part of a broader shift in the discipline, represented in the work of Barth, 1966; Bailey, 1960; Swartz, Turner, and Tuden, 1966; and Epstein, 1967. For an overview of this move in anthropology, see Ortner, 1984; and see Giddens, 1979 for a more general discussion of the tension between agency and structure in social analysis.

25. For a discussion of this shift, see Snyder, 1981, p. 145.

26. Epstein, 1967; Van Velsen, 1967.

27. Comaroff and Roberts, 1981, p.14.

28. See, for example, Aubert, 1963; Gulliver, 1963; Eckhoff, 1966; Nader, 1969; Collier, 1973; Starr and Yngvesson, 1975; Starr, 1978; and more generally, Nader and Todd, 1978.

29. Ortner, 1984, p. 151.

30. Comaroff and Roberts, 1981, p. 17.

31. Nader, 1969; Collier, 1973, p. 59.

32. Nader, 1969, p. 90. For a related discussion, see Emerson, 1983.

33. Collier, 1973, p. 13.

34. Yngvesson, 1976.

35. Moore, 1972, pp. 75 and 90.

36. At the same time, discussion of these longer-term developments is often framed in the language of choice and strategy. For example: "The group decision when it is opportune to expand, or the group decision that there has been an encroachment which must be resisted, is in some (not all) ways analogous to the decisions of individuals to advance themselves at the expense of others, or to react to the self-seeking of others. On both levels there are many choices" (Moore, 1972, p. 76).

37. Yngvesson, 1976; Mather and Yngvesson, 1980-1981; Felstiner, Abel, and Sarat, 1980-1981; Yngvesson, 1984; Greenhouse, 1986.

38. The distinction between "dispute processes" and "dispute processing" is not always clear, and the latter (which tends to be used by academic lawyers to describe the procedural forms by which disputes are handled) can be seen as a dimension of the former. But as Snyder notes, dispute processing research tends to be instrumentalist "and is often devoted to the extension of state control and the implementation of practical, procedural reforms" (Snyder, 1981, pp. 146–147). Dispute processing research has appropriated and domesticated anthropological theory on disputing to advocate forums for "neighborhood justice" in which lay mediators attempt to "settle" disputes informally (see Merry, 1982). This literature (and these lay practices) have been influential in affirming and perpetuating an ideology of state law as distinct from local, "unofficial" procedures that are represented as a form of

popular or "community" justice abstracted from state power. For a critique of the "alternative" dispute resolution movement, see Merry, 1987 and Yngvesson, 1988a. For a discussion of the ideology of "community" justice, see Yngvesson, 1993.

39. Cain and Kulcsar, 1981–82, p. 397 (emphasis in original).

40. See in particular Cain and Kulcsar, 1981–1982, p. 389.

41. Moore, 1972, p. 77.

42. Mitchell, 1990, p. 565.

43. Ibid., p. 566; and see Mitchell's discussion of culture on pp. 559–561.

44. It is interesting to compare the distinction of "interpersonal" disputes (specified as, for example, marital, neighbor, and other matters) and structural conflict, by critics of the disputing paradigm such as Cain and Kulcsar, and the parallel distinction between neighborhood and family disturbances, on the one hand, and property crime, on the other, made by criminal court personnel and police. In both, the distinction maintains an ideological separation of personal and structural, of that which is relevant to public order and that which is not, although for quite different ends.

45. See Fantasia's discussion of "emergent culture" (1988, pp. 17–18); and see Raymond Williams, 1977, pp. 112–114 for a discussion of the openness of cultural processes.

46. See Bourdieu, 1987, p. 234.

47. See, for example, Eisenstein and Jacob, 1977; Feeley, 1979; Mather, 1979; Maynard, 1988.

48. Mather, 1974, p. 286. Mather uses this phrase to describe defense attorneys and defendants who opt for a more traditional adversary role in courtroom litigation rather than bargaining for a reduced sentence by submitting a guilty plea. Most defense attorneys prefer to seek a disposition that minimizes the sentence for a client, and this requires that the attorney "should represent the client by doing what was best for him, rather than simply by implementing what the client wanted." I am using the phrase somewhat more broadly than she does, to suggest the limited role of nonprofessionals in most courtroom decisionmaking. Mather's analysis of "maverick" defense attorneys suggests, however, that the boundary between "insiders" and "outsiders" is blurred and shifting. "Mavericks" are attorneys who accept a client's view of appropriate strategy, and while very few of the defense attorneys Mather studied fell into this category, those who did were among the more senior members of the public defender office.

49. The concept of "normal trouble" is discussed in Sudnow, 1965 and Emerson, 1969, pp. 83–100.

50. See, for example, O'Barr and Conley, 1985; Sarat and Felstiner, 1986; Maynard, 1988.

51. Harrington, 1985, p. 147.

52. From an official legal perspective, criminal courts do not deal with true "legal" matters at all (by definition, issues of central structural importance in society) but with social messes involving the most peripheral individuals and groups (see Harrington, ibid., pp. 146–147; McBarnet, 1981).

53. See, for example, Engel, 1984; Greenhouse, 1986, 1988; Greenhouse, Engel, and Yngvesson, 1993 for a discussion of these "ways of life."

54. Black, 1980, p. 239, quoting Shurtleff, 1853, p. 92.

55. Baumgartner, 1985; Merry and Silbey, 1984, p. 151; Greenhouse, 1988, pp. 702–704.

56. See Moore, 1982, pp. 55–56; and Fitzpatrick, 1988.

Notes to Chapter 2

1. *Greenfield Recorder*, May 12, 1983, p. 3.
2. See infra, p. 17 for a discussion of the show cause hearing.
3. Several dispositions are possible for misdemeanor charges in Massachusetts district courts, including a sentence, a suspended sentence, a fine, probation, and "continued without a finding," which is the least serious disposition, and does not result in a criminal record (that is, the case is dismissed following a continuance period).
4. Springfield is the largest city in the region, about an hour drive to the south.
5. Interview, docket, and observational data suggest that the police are typically called before complainants go to the court in conflicts involving family members, neighbors, and acquaintances. Of the 95 family and neighbor complaints filed by citizens with the district court clerk in Franklin County between June 1 and December 31, 1982, 81 specifically mentioned at least 1 (and some up to 10) calls to the police before the complaint was brought to court.
6. See Massachusetts General Laws, chapter 218, section 26. The distinction between misdemeanors and felonies is based on definitions of seriousness, which include (but are not restricted to) consideration of the amount of harm caused. Harm may be measured in terms of amount of injury or value of property destroyed or taken. For example, "assault" may be either a misdemeanor or a felony, depending on the extent of injury, and "shoplifting" is a misdemeanor, while "breaking and entering" involving theft of valuable property is generally a felony. Seriousness may also be determined by considerations such as *when* an offense was committed (e.g., breaking and entering during the night is more serious than breaking and entering during the day). Murder, rape, and burglary are felonies and are punishable by imprisonment in a state institution or by death; misdemeanors are typically punished by a fine, a suspended sentence, or imprisonment in a county jail. The lines between misdemeanors and felonies are not clearly drawn, however, and the negotiation of seriousness that I describe in complaint hearings is a key feature of the definitional process that occurs at other stages of the criminal process as well. See, generally, Harrington, 1985, pp. 144–149 for a discussion about the "value" of minor disputes in municipal courts, and see Mather, 1979, for a discussion of bargaining about seriousness in felony court.
7. Massachusetts General Laws Ann., chapter 218, section 35A, p. 55.
8. Administrative Office of the District Court Department, *Standards of Judicial Practice*, 1975, 3:00; and see Committee on Juries of Six, 1984, p. 74
9. Ibid.; and see Harrington, 1985, pp. 145–149 for a general discussion of "garbage" as "the work of the lower courts" (ibid., p. 147).
10. These phrases are ones that are used regularly by staff in the Franklin County court to describe citizen-signed complaint applications.
11. The 617 complaints described in Table 2.1 include all applications for a criminal complaint filed by citizens and town police from 18 villages and towns in Franklin County during the period June 1–December 31, 1982. These figures do not include motor vehicle complaints (including fuel tax complaints) brought by state police; nor do they include non-support complaints or complaints of welfare fraud brought by the Department of Public Welfare. See n.22, Chapter 5 for a discussion of these complaints.

12. Of 92 denials of citizen complaints at the Franklin County court, 40% (37) were "issued technically," "held at the show cause level," or "continued for a few months."

13. I am defining "work" here in terms of caseload, since this is the criterion used officially for measuring court work. The total non-motor-vehicle criminal caseload of the Franklin County District Court for fiscal year 1982 was 1518 complaints. I estimate that the clerk's office handled over 1000 complaint applications by citizens and police during this same period (based on the 618 complaint applications in my 7-month sample).

14. Emerson and Messinger, 1977, p. 123.

15. Ibid., pp. 127–128.

16. See Mather and Yngvesson (1980–1981) for a discussion of the ways that audiences shape the public meaning of dispute.

17. Pierre Bourdieu, 1977, p. 5, notes the relationship between "so-called objective truth . . . and the truth that can scarcely be called subjective, since it represents the official definition of the subjective experience of the exchange."

18. The clerks at the Franklin County court commented repeatedly on this practice, associating it with the "withdrawal" of other agencies from their responsibility in handling neighborhood and family problems. See note 5, p. 17, for discussion of early police involvement in complaints brought to the clerk by citizens.

19. See discussion of these exchanges in Chapters 4 and 5.

20. See discussion in Chapter 4.

21. For example, in the series of complaints from Turners Falls described in Chapter 6, the clerk advised one complainant that "You know, if this goes to court, none of the peripheral issues—about noise, disturbances, disagreements—are going to be admitted into evidence." When one complainant introduced a map in order to define neighborhood fighting in the context of trespass, the clerk brushed it aside as "not crucial" (see pp. 89–90).

22. Charges of neighborhood noise, for example, imply that complainants assume unlimited rights to the enjoyment of their property, while the clerks repeatedly talk about limits to these rights. See discussion in Chapter 4, and see Merry, 1990, p. 45, and Brigham, 1988.

23. Bourdieu, 1977, p. 40.

24. Ibid.

25. See discussion, infra, pp. 28–29.

26. Pocock, 1985, p. 112.

27. Pocock, 1985, pp. 103–104, describes property both as "that which makes you what you are" and "that to which you have a right," in the western political tradition; it is "an extension and a pre-requisite of personality." And see Merry, 1990, pp. 44–47 for a discussion of the importance of property as a theme in neighbor conflicts. Brigham, 1988, provides a more general discussion of the meaning of property rights in American legal culture.

28. See Chapter 7.

29. Santos, 1987, p. 298.

30. Bourdieu, 1987, p. 229. Bourdieu argues that "law is the quintessential form of 'active' discourse, able by its own operation to produce its effects" (ibid., p. 234). See Mather and Yngvesson, 1980–1981, pp. 783–797, on the significance of third parties in this process; and see Emerson and Messinger, supra, note 14.

31. Bourdieu, 1987, p. 229.

32. The concept of "potential space" is developed by D.W. Winnicott (1971, pp. 41, 47, 107ff.) in a discussion of creativity and of play. According to Winnicott, creativity is made possible by the ambiguous relational status of baby to mother at a developmental moment when the baby feels both separate from the mother and attached to her. I draw on this insight to theorize the creative potential of the court clerk's ambiguous position vis-à-vis the law. See infra pp. 29–30. For further discussion of Winnicott's position, see Phillips, pp. 121–126, 1988 and Mahoney and Yngvesson, 1992.

33. Smith, 1961, pp. 81,84.

34. Ibid., pp. 103–128, 159.

35. Hartog, 1976, pp. 287–313.

36. Ibid., p. 284. Until the late eighteenth century, the criminal practice of the sessions court "was less a part of a province-wide system of criminal justice than a repository of power for the use of a county government. By the same token, much of its administrative practice was marked by a quasi-criminal manner of procedure" (ibid., p. 323). See also Haskins' comment that in seventeenth-century England, "[i]t is extraordinary how much of English local government could be, and was, carried on through the forms of criminal trial" (1984, p. 54).

37. A detailed discussion of the role of sessions courts and of the elite status of the magistracy is provided in Snell, 1970. See also Haskins, 1960, pp. 24–42; and Smith, 1961. For a discussion of the broad jurisdiction of sessions courts, see Hartog, 1976, p. 285. Smith, discussing the Pynchon Court Record for the Court of General Sessions of the Peace for Hampshire in the last decade of the seventeenth century, notes that the "outstanding feature [of the Record] is the flexibility of administration, both in taking jurisdiction without seeking support in the letter of the laws and in awarding punishment" (1961, p. 127; and see Smith, pp. 83–84, for the list of violations that justices of the peace were authorized "to hear and determine" in the Second Charter of 1692).

38. Hartog, 1976, p. 291, and see pp. 318–323. Similar complaints are described in Smith, 1961, pp. 113–115; Konig, 1979, pp. 55–57, 70–72; and in Boyer and Nissenbaum, 1974, p. 125. There is an extensive literature on law in the colonial period that points to the complex linkage between the "peace" made by local magistrates and the politics of community in local settings. See, e.g., Haskins, 1960; Nelson, 1981; Black, 1980; Goebel and Naughton, 1944; and Greenberg, 1976. This literature suggests that self-discipline, "holy watching" by members of a congregation, and intervention by church elders or magistrates in a broad range of everyday social and economic relations were interwoven, especially in the early colonial period (see Haskins, 1960, pp. 60–65). It also points however to the diversity of the colonists, and to economic and religious tensions that were fought out in county courts and before town selectmen, which thus became arenas in which "magistrates and complainants shaped standards of fairness, defined concepts of 'right,' and forged a legal culture in which the magistracy became a prominent moral force in local communities" (Yngvesson, 1989, p. 1698); and see Jones, 1984, pp. 153–190.

39. Nelson, 1981, p. 70; and see Hartog, 1976, p. 324, for a discussion of the political context and social implications of these reforms, in which "there was no place for a discretionary problem-solver that was not tied to the sovereign people of the whole Commonwealth."

40. See Provine, 1986, pp. 24–60 on the transformation and elimination of lay magistrates.

41. Hartog, 1976, p. 325.

42. See Provine, 1986, pp. 1–60 for a discussion of this process. In particular, Provine notes the opposition to courts and lawyers in Shay's Rebellion (1786) in western Massachusetts, and the "simmering popular resentment against legal profession [sic] and the increasingly lawyer-dominated courts" (1986, p. 12). And see Botein, 1981.

43. Nelson, 1981, p. 69; Ellis, 1971, pp. 198-224.

44. Taylor, 1954, pp. 111–121; Starkey, 1955.

45. Horowitz, 1977, pp. 22–23, 140–159.

46. See Jenkins, 1982, pp. 49–72, for a discussion of the connections of Greenfield's economic development to the emergence of what he terms a "dynasty" of lawyers in the town at the end of the eighteenth century. For a general discussion of the development of a translocal community of lawyers and businessmen in nineteenth-century America, see Bender, 1978, pp. 86–120; and see Auerbach, 1983, pp. 95–147.

47. Jenkins, 1982, pp. 58–59.

48. Bender, 1978, pp. 87–93.

49. For a discussion of "high"/"low" distinctions, see Stalleybrass and White, 1986, pp. 1–5. Popular culture is interpreted as a site of struggle in de Certeau (1984) and Stalleybrass and White (1986, pp. 27-79); and see Chapter 6.

50. Max Weber uses this phrase to describe the bureaucratic administration of justice. (Weber, 1967, p. 351).

51. Keebler, 1930, p. 12, quoted in Provine, 1986, p. 40 (and see her note 63, p. 210).

52. Tocqueville, 1850 (1969), p. 264.

53. Horowitz, 1977, p. 22.

54. Lane, 1967, pp. 3–38.

55. Vanlandingham, 1964, p. 44, quoting a Washington Supreme Court justice.

56. Steinberg, 1984, pp. 573, 581; Hartog, 1976, p. 326; and see more generally Provine, 1986, pp. 26–29; Harrington, 1982, p. 46; and Wickersham Commission, 1931, pp. 3–10.

57. Steinberg, 1989, p.17, quoting prison Agent William J. Mullen, a reformer who joined the Philadelphia court system in 1850 in order to check private prosecutions.

58. Harrington, 1982, p.42 (citing R. H. Smith, 1919; Scott, 1923; and Maguire, 1926; and see Provine's discussion of the Progressive movement to reform rural justice (1986, pp. 34–42).

59. Vanlandingham, 1964, p. 43, citing an attorney in a Kentucky mountain county.

60. President's Commission on Law Enforcement and Administration of Justice, 1967, p. 324, citing a Report by a Virginia Committee to Study Problems of Justices of the Peace.

61. Provine, 1986, p. 34, citing Tumey v. Ohio, 1927, p. 532. Similarly, the reliance on juries was seen as rendering laws "'which ought to be an uniform rule of conduct, uncertain, fluctuating with every change of passion and opinion of jurors, and impossible to be known till pronounced'" (Horowitz, 1977, p. 28, citing a statement of a judge in 1792).

62. Weber, 1967, p. 351.

63. Steinberg, 1989, p. 9.

64. Ibid., p. 14. For a related argument, see Gordon, 1988, pp. 250–299.

Gordon describes the ways abused women sought to control family violence through complaints to social workers in Boston child-saving agencies between 1880 and 1960, arguing that it was through these complaints that women invented "a right not to be beaten" (1988, p. 258).

65. Platt, 1969.

66. For a parallel account, see Natalie Zemon Davis' discussion of the place of letters of remission in the empowerment of king, notaries, and supplicants in sixteenth-century France (1987). Davis describes the "complicity between sovereign and subject" in letters of remission, arguing that "in the field between the true and the plausible, royal grace and power could grow, and supplicants could harvest restored life and good name" (1987, p. 58).

67. Wickersham Commission, 1931, pp. 7–8.

68. Committee on Juries of Six, 1984, p. 74.

69. Wickersham Commission, 1931, p. 9.

70. Weber, 1967, p. 351.

71. The ideology of detached professionalism that was central to the reform movement excluded "farmers, blacksmiths, carpenters, shoemakers, plumbers, and every conceivable kind of laborer and tradesman . . . [from] the bench of a court of justice" (Provine, 1986, p. 31, quoting C. Smith, 1927). See also Harrington and Merry, 1988, p. 730, for a discussion of how mediation processes "defined as neutral and interpreted as requiring a detached stance" produce a core of mediators who "tend to be people with higher education and professional training for whom the detached stance is a learned professional demeanor and approach." Mediators who come from the working class communities whose problems are handled by neighborhood justice programs find a detached stance "unnatural" and are used less often.

72. Committee of Juries of Six, 1984, p. 75.

73. Wickersham Commission, 1931, p. 8.

74. See above, pp. 21–23. The construction of assaults as "personal," while property matters are privileged as matters of public concern is part of an ideology of property as the basis of social life that is rooted in seventeenth century conceptions of civic virtue as grounded in propertied independence (Pocock, 1985, pp. 66,69).

75. Harrington, 1982, p. 46 quoting a statement by Herbert Harley, founder and secretary of the American Judicature Society, in 1915 (Harley, 1915, p. 513).

76. McDermott, 1983, p. 12.

77. Ibid., p. 22.

78. Massachusetts General Laws, chapter 218, section 8.

79. See interpretation of complaint management policy by the head clerk at the Franklin County District Court, Chapter 5.

80. See Harrington, 1982, pp. 47–49 for an analysis of this concept and its accompanying rationale, that it would "democratize" the lower courts. In the Court Reorganization Act (1978 Massachusetts Acts, chapter 478, section 324), district courts became "divisions" of the Trial Court of the Commonwealth; budgetary responsibility for each court was transferred from local counties to the Commonwealth, and procedures for screening and redirecting "local" conflicts were tightened. And see General Laws, chapter 211B, section 10. Harrington, 1982, pp. 47–49 analyzes the implications of unification of the court system during the progressive era, as a means of controlling marshalls, and particularly court clerks, who were viewed by

reformers as "'partially independent functionaries over whom courts [had] little real control'" (1982, p. 48, citing American Bar Association, 1909, p. 591).

81. Massachusetts General Laws, chapter 218, section 35A (amended by St. 1978, chapter 478, section 193) provides that "If a complaint for a misdemeanor is received by a district court, or by a justice, associate justice or special justice thereof, or by a clerk, assistant clerk, temporary clerk or temporary assistant clerk thereof . . . the court, or any of said officers . . . shall, unless there is an imminent threat of bodily injury, of the commission of a crime or of flight from the commonwealth by the person against whom such complaint is made, give to said person, if not under arrest for the offense for which the complaint is made, notice in writing of such complaint; *and said person shall be given an opportunity to be heard in opposition to the issuance of process*" (emphasis added). See also Cowin, 1978.

82. Committee on Juries of Six, 1984, p. 74.

83. See Santos, 1977, pp. 99–101, and Mather and Yngvesson, 1980–1981, pp. 782, 810–817 for a discussion of the "relevant community" or the "relevant audience."

84. This process is reminiscent of de Tocqueville's insight that in America "the spirit of the law . . . infiltrates through society right down to the lowest ranks, till finally the whole people have contracted some of the ways and tastes of a magistrate. Law . . . has no banner of its own; it adapts itself flexibly to the exigencies of the moment and lets itself be carried along unresistingly by every movement of the body social; but it enwraps the whole of society, penetrating each component class and constantly working in secret upon its unconscious patient, till in the end it has molded it to its desire" [Tocqueville, 1850 (1969), p. 270].

85. Bourdieu, 1977, p. 163.

86. Standards of Judicial Practice, 1975, p. 3:17.

87. Ibid., p. 3:00.

88. Bourdieu, 1987, p. 229, argues that "the specific power of legal professionals consists in *revealing* rights—and revealing injustices by the same process—or, on the contrary, in vetoing feelings of injustice based on a sense of fairness alone and, thereby, in discouraging the legal defense of subjective rights." See also his discussion of the power of naming, pp. 233 ff.

89. See discussion in Chapter 5.

90. For example, a "garbage" complaint about borrowed dime store rings was used by one clerk in Franklin County to argue that a formal charge of crime should be issued against the teenager involved, who had "run" from her foster home. In this case, "garbage" *became* a crime so that the teenager could be apprehended (Yngvesson, 1988, pp. 441–442). And see Chapter 5, p. 72.

91. de Certeau, 1984, pp. 18, 26.

92. Bourdieu, 1987, p. 229. I draw here on Peter Fitzpatrick's analysis of the politics of alternative law (1988, pp. 190–197) to push the implications of the legal power of "naming" beyond the limits of Bourdieu's discussion.

93. Winnicott, 1971, p. 101 (emphasis in original). Winnicott makes this point in a discussion of cultural experience as located "in the *potential space* between the individual and the environment," and suggests that it is in this space that creativity is possible as "the new" is simultaneously "found" and "created" (1971, p. 100, and see pp. 88–89). While Winnicott is discussing issues of separateness and union in the maturational process of infants, his

analysis of the paradox of creativity as simultaneously an invention and a discovery of what is "already there" has implications for the explanation of what Bourdieu terms "juridicization" or "officialization" (Bourdieu, 1987, p. 232 and 1977, pp. 164–171). Bourdieu argues that while law "creates the social world" we must remember "that it is this world which first *creates* the law . . . . Our thought categories *contribute* to the production of the world, but only within the limits of their correspondence with preexisting structures." Thus "the will to transform the world by transforming the words for naming it, by producing new categories of perception and judgment, and by dictating a new vision of social divisions and distributions, can only succeed if the resulting prophecies, or creative evocations, are also, at least in part, well-founded *previsions*, anticipatory descriptions" (1987, pp. 234–235, emphasis in original). For a theoretical account of agency that explains the relationship of invention to reproduction, see Mahoney and Yngvesson, 1992.

94. Stalleybrass and White, 1986, p. 194. Stalleybrass and White, in a broad historical overview, are discussing the grouping of sites of discursive production through which bourgeois identity is constituted, and specifically the hierarchy of places of production (court, church, marketplace, tavern, fair) through which subjects define themselves by excluding the repulsive and contaminating.

95. See Chapter 3, p. 43.

96. Today, the memory of this counterconvention remains alive as the "long history of independent mindedness" going back to Shay's Rebellion, "when a band of impoverished farmers took pitchforks and guns and headed down from the hills to protest high taxes." This event was used to constitute the meaning of a contemporary rebellion, when five Massachusetts "hilltowns" refused in the spring of 1991 to pay off state loans for school projects (*The New York Times*, May 19, 1991, p. 14).

Notes to Chapter 3

1. The takebacks included a 7% pay cut, rollback of fringe benefits, cutting paid sick days and 2 of 13 paid holidays, and a stipulation that future increases in group insurance premiums would be paid by employees (*Greenfield Recorder*, March 31, 1983, p. 1).

2. *Greenfield Recorder*, August 11, 1983, p. 12.

3. *Greenfield Recorder*, May 11, 1983, p. 9, in a letter written by Judith Ruff, president of United Electrical, Radio and Machine Workers of America (UE) Local 274.

4. *Greenfield Recorder*, November 19, 1982, p. 14, quoting John B.Hostettler, manager of the job matching service at the state Division of Employment Security in Greenfield.

5. *Greenfield Recorder*, August 15, 1983, p. 10.

6 *Greenfield Recorder*, February 8, 1983, p. 8.

7. *Greenfield Recorder*, March 23, 1982, p. 1, quoting candidate for town selectman Gary T. Oberg's statement that for Greenfield to "grow and prosper," an override of proposition 2 1/2, industrial development, and good town management were needed.

8. See Selectmen's Annual Report to the town of Greenfield, 1895, quoted above, p. 32.

9. Interview with Greenfield resident, quoted in Jenkins, 1982, p. 15.

10. Ibid., pp. 3–5.

11. *Greenfield Recorder*, May 3, 1983, p. 1.

12. *Greenfield Recorder*, October 15, 1983, p. 3, quoting Ronald M. Ansin, commissioner of the state Department of Commerce and Development in an address to the Franklin County Chamber of Commerce.

13. *Greenfield Recorder*, January 24, 1983, p. 1, quoting Lewis Goetz.

14. *Greenfield Recorder*, June 25, 1983, p. 3, quoting Alex Markley.

15. Jenkins, 1982, p. 136.

16. Cited in Jenkins, 1982, p. 134. This discussion of the development of the tap and die industry is based on Jenkins, pp. 134–143.

17. Ibid., p. 181.

18. *Greenfield Recorder*, October 3, 1983, p. 11. The words are those of a Franklin County resident who contributed an article to the "Reader's Report" section of the newspaper.

19. Ibid.

20. *Greenfield Recorder*, January 24, 1983, p. 1; and Greenfield Recorder, November 3, 1983, p. 3

21. *Greenfield Recorder*, July 2, 1982, p. 3.

22. Ibid., quoting R. John Ryan, Jr.

23. *Greenfield Recorder*, July 16, 1982, p. 1, quoting Ann L. Hamilton.

24. Ibid., citing concerns expressed by Don A. Aikens, junior warden for St. James Episcopal Church.

25. Ibid., pp. 12 and 1, quoting Empire One official Tina Beauvais and a local attorney representing the corporation.

26. Ibid., p. 12, quoting Frank S. Roche.

27. Ibid., p. 1.

28. Collier et al., 1982, p. 36.

29. See, for example, Engel, 1984 and 1987; Greenhouse, 1986, pp. 74–181, and 1988; Boyer and Nissenbaum, 1974, pp. 80–109 and 179–216. For a more general discussion of market and community as competing interpretive frameworks, see Bender, 1978, pp. 45–120 (especially 113–120). For a particularly insightful discussion of the tension between perceptions of public credit as corruption (in that it was seen as creating dependence on government by creditors and vice versa) and seventeenth-century ideologies of agrarian virtue (as independence through property ownership), see Pocock, 1985, pp. 51–71.

30. The discussion of Greenfield history in this section draws primarily on Jenkins, 1982, pp. 9–115. Jenkins' account, commissioned by the town and thus an officially sanctioned portrayal of the past, has particular relevance for my interest in how local populations imagine themselves, and in how these visions inform current contests about "community" and its demise.

31. Ibid., p. 108.

32. Ibid., p. 95. For a more general discussion of hostility to lawyers in early America, see Provine, 1986, pp. 9–17 and Gawalt, 1970.

33. See Chapter 6 for an analysis of this struggle in Turners Falls.

34. Quoted in Jenkins, 1982, pp. 129–130, and see generally Jenkins, 1982, pp. 98–131 for a discussion of the local significance of the development of Turners Falls.

35. Ibid., p. 185, and see discussion on pp. 181–187.

36. See description of tap and die, p. 34.

37. Jenkins, 1982, p. 137.

38. Ibid., p. 142.
39. Ibid., pp. 135.
40. Ibid., p. 213. Jenkins quotes an interview taped in 1975 with the personnel manager of Millers Falls Co. in support of this representation of a factory as family.
41. Ibid., 221.
42. *Greenfield Recorder*, August 25, 1983, p. 1. The settlement froze wages for a year, provided for a 30 to 35-cent hourly raise in the second and third years, and maintained fringe benefits provided by the last contract.
43. Ibid.
44. Moore, 1977.
45. Turner, 1974, p. 35.
46. *Greenfield Recorder*, May 18, 1983, p. 1.
47. Ibid.
48. *Greenfield Recorder*, November 6, 1982, pp. 1, 10.
49. Ibid., p. 10.
50. Bourdieu, 1977, p. 171.
51. For a parallel discussion of family ideology and market economy, see Collier, Rosaldo, and Yanagisako, 1982, pp. 34–35.
52. Center for Massachusetts Data, *Census of Population and Housing*, 1980, p. 4, Table 29.
53. Ibid.
54. Ibid., Summary Level 16, ED21T (p. 7, Table 51; p. 8, Table 59); ED21U (p. 7, Table 51; p. 8, Table 59); ED18 (p. 7, Table 51; p. 8, Table 59).
55. Ibid., Summary Level 16, ED21T, Tables 5, 11, 14. See Appendix 2 for figures.
56. Bourdieu, 1977, p. 191. Bourdieu uses this phrase in a discussion of what he calls domination "in its elementary form, i.e. directly, between one person and another" (emphasis in original deleted).
57. For a discussion of the broader implications of this theme in American culture, see Greenhouse, Yngvesson, and Engel (1993).
58. The term "brainless" was used by some court staff to describe complaints that court staff felt could have been resolved without a court appearance, had the parties involved exercised more self-control. See discussion supra, Chapter 2, pp. 17–18.
59. Jenkins, 1982, pp. 58, 59; and see p. 134, for a discussion of the use of the courthouse as a secret meeting place for planners of a short-lived strike in Greenfield in 1870.
60. County Commisioners, 1980–1981, p. 3.
61. *Greenfield Recorder*, February 17, 1983, p. 16.
62. *Greenfield Recorder*, February 18, 1983, p. 10.
63. Ibid.
64. Ibid., February 15, 1983, p. 1.
65. Massachusetts General Laws, Chapter 211B (10); and see Chapter 2, pp. 28–29.
66. *Greenfield Recorder*, December 29, 1982, p. 12.
67. Walzer, 1963, pp. 79–82.
68. *Greenfield Recorder*, July 29, 1983, p. 12.
69. See Chapter 2, pp. 28–29.
70. Hartog, 1976, p. 291.
71. Turner, 1957, pp. 91–93 developed this concept to discuss patterned

eruptions of conflict with what he termed a "processional form." Turner's concept of factional struggles as providing "a limited area of transparency on the otherwise opaque surface of regular, uneventful social life" (p. 93) is helpful in my analysis of a series of neighborhood confrontations that were staged at the Franklin County courthouse (see Chapter 6). Ginsburg's expanded use of the "social drama" in her discussion of conflicts between pro-life and pro-choice activists in Fargo, North Dakota suggests that people involved in social dramas are also rewriting the script as they enact it (Ginsburg, 1989, pp. 62–75). This move is helpful in adapting Turner's processual model to the explanation of social transformation, but could go further in this direction by moving away from Turner's conceptual orientation [that is, his emphasis on "models . . . carried in the actors' heads" (Turner, 1974, p. 36, cited in Ginsburg, 1989, p. 63)] to a more practice-oriented analysis, such as that implied by Fantasia's (1988, pp. 16–17) discussion of the embodiment of consciousness in "cultures of solidarity", a formulation that also draws on Turner's work. I discuss this issue in greater detail in Chapter 6.

Notes to Chapter 4

1. Foucault, 1982, p. 220. In elaborating this notion of power, Foucault notes the subtlety of the term *conduct*, as meaning both "to lead" and as "a way of behaving within a more or less open field of possibilities. The exercise of power consists in guiding the possibility of conduct and putting in order the possible outcome. Basically power is less a confrontation between two adversaries or the linking of one to the other than a question of government. . . . To govern . . . is to structure the possible field of action of others" (pp. 220–221).

2. Giddens, 1979, p. 93 (emphasis in original). Comaroff and Comaroff (1991, p. 22) distinguish agentive and nonagentive modes of power, describing the former as "command wielded by human beings in specific historical contexts," and the latter as hidden "in the forms of everyday life" (see also Lukes, 1974, esp. pp. 21–25). My discussion of the court clerk's capacity to govern links these two forms of power. The clerk's governing capacity (that is, his capacity for command) is enabled (and depends on) what "goes without saying" (Bourdieu, 1977, p. 170).

3. See Bourdieu, 1977, pp. 1–9.

4. Ibid., 1.

5. Foucault, 1982, p. 220.

6. Bourdieu, 1977, pp. 6–9.

7. Administrative Office of the District Court Department, *Standards of Judicial Practice*, 1975, p. 3:00.

8. Ibid., pp. 3:00, 3:15. Attorneys "have no right to put questions to participants directly and should be permitted to participate only to the extent that the magistrate feels it will be materially helpful in deciding whether process should issue" (p. 3:15). The limited provision made for attorney participation in complaint hearings reflects the perception of the bar that use of trained professionals for minor criminal and civil matters—"typical municipal court cases," traffic complaints, small claims, and the like—is "a waste" (Provine, 1986, p. 49, citing a 1971 ABA-sponsored study of lawyer judges in California).

9. Ibid., p. 3:00. The term "magistrate" is used in the District Courts to mean "District Court personnel authorized by law to issue criminal process, i.e. a Justice, Special Justice, Clerk, Temporary Clerk, Assistant Clerk or Temporary Assistant Clerk" (Ibid., p. 1:01; and see Massachusetts General Laws, Chapter 218, Sections 32, 33, 35).

10. Ibid., p. 3:17.

11. Court clerks can be either male or female. The language of the Massachusetts General Laws, and all of the official documents used in this research, presume a male clerk, however, as indicated by the exclusive use of male pronouns. All of the (5) clerks in Franklin and Essex counties were male.

12. Bittner, 1969, p. 172.

13. Ibid., pp. 170–171; and see Michael Banton, 1964, pp. 6–7 and 127ff.

14. Bittner, 1969, pp. 181–183.

15. Bittner, 1974, pp. 32–34.

16. See Appendix for list of charges filed in Franklin County.

17. During 15 months of research in Franklin County and at the District Court of Essex, I observed five different clerks, two in Franklin County and three in Essex. At the Essex court, hearings were typically held in the clerk's office, although occasionally they were moved to a conference room if a large number of participants was involved. In Franklin County, hearings were almost always held in a courtroom.

18. In fiscal year 1982, 27,989 criminal complaints were filed at the District Court of Essex in Salem (91%, or 25,333 of these, were motor vehicle complaints). Only the district court in Worcester, with a criminal caseload of 29,520, had a larger caseload than Salem. (The Boston Municipal Court does not appear in reports of district court statistics.) (Administrative Office of District Courts, 1982).

19. The criminal caseload of the Franklin County District Court for fiscal year 1982 was 2872 [of which 41% (1354 cases) were motor vehicle complaints]. (Administrative Office of District Courts, 1982). See footnote 18 for Essex County figures.

20. Santos, 1987, p. 297.

21. Bourdieu, 1987, pp. 179, 192. Bourdieu describes the "gentle, invisible form of violence, which is never recognized as such, and is not so much undergone as chosen, the violence of credit, confidence, obligation, personal loyalty, hospitality, gifts, gratitude, piety" (p. 192).

22. Most citizens are unrepresented in complaint hearings. An attorney was present in only 19% (57) of the 293 complaints brought by private citizens in Franklin County between June and December 1982. In 23 of these, both parties were represented, in 22 only the defendant was represented, while in 12 only the complainant was represented. I do not have comparable data for the Essex court, but attorneys were rarely present at hearings I attended. In both courts, the presence of an attorney altered the dynamics of the exchange significantly, either in eclipsing the role of the clerk (at the Essex court) or through a collaboration with him (in Franklin County).

23. Atkinson and Drew, 1979, pp. 61–62.

24. See Mather and Yngvesson, 1980–1981 for a discussion of how the reframing of trouble by third parties reproduces power relations; and see Bourdieu's (1987, p. 229) discussion of the power of legal professionals as located in "*revealing* rights—and revealing injustices by the same process—or, on the contrary, in vetoing feelings of injustice based on a

sense of fairness alone and, thereby, in discouraging the legal defense of subjective rights."

25. Fantasia, 1988, p. 174.

26. Giddens, 1979, p. 57; and see Raymand Williams' discussion of "lived hegemony" (1977, p. 112).

27. Foucault, 1982, p. 221. See discussion supra, pp. 47–48 and footnote 1, above.

28. See discussion of the tension built into the clerk's position as magistrate, Chapter 2, pp. 29–30.

29. Bourdieu, describing the relationship of the ethnographer to what she studies, notes how "exaltation of the virtues of the distance secured by externality simply transmutes into an epistemological choice the anthropologist's objective situation, that of "impartial spectator," as Husserl puts it, condemned to see all practice as spectacle." In this hearing, the clerk, too, "withdrew," constituting the activity before him as "an object of observation and analysis, a representation" (1977, pp. 1–2).

30. See Chapter 6.

31. Bourdieu, 1977, p. 1.

32. For a discussion of this displacement at the Salem court, see Merry, 1990, esp. pp. 110ff.

33. See discussion of "potential space" in Chapter 2, pp. 24, 30, and see Winnicott, 1971, pp. 41, 47, 107ff.

34. See Chapter 2 for a discussion of the emergence of these distinctions with the professionalization of law in nineteenth-century America. More detailed discussion of the distinction, particularly as it is found in the Essex court, is provided in Chapter 5.

Notes to Chapter 5

1. Douglas, 1966, p. 48.

2. See discussion in Chapter 2, pp. 27–29.

3. Bourdieu (1987, p. 224) describes the institution of a "judicial space" as setting up a borderline that divides specialists from nonspecialists in terms of their "view of the case." The "vulgar vision" is that of the client or nonspecialist, and the "professional vision" is that of the lawyer or judge.

4. Statements about this court refer only to the period 1981–1982, when this research was in progress.

5. Actual mediation sessions are conducted elsewhere, but the program, like other similar ones throughout the United States, is closely linked to the court. See, generally, Harrington and Merry 1988, for a discussion of the ideology of mediation, and Abel, 1982 for a more general critique of informal justice, which is widely regarded as simply another mechanism for expanding state power.

6. These are terms used by court personnel to describe complaints.

7. "A and B" refers to assault and battery.

8. Of 882 complaints filed with the Essex clerk during 6 months in 1981 and 1982, 33% (290) were filed by citizens, 46% (407) by businesses, 18% (158) by agencies, and 3% (27) by the police. "Checks and DPW" refers to bad check complaints filed by businesses and nonsupport or fraud complaints filed by the Department of Public Welfare, a frequent agency complainant. Between March 1 and May 18, 1981, and between February 1 and May 1,

1982, 39% (346) of 882 complaints filed with the clerk were for larceny by check; of these 95% (328) were brought by local businesses. There was an increase in larceny by check cases between 1981 and 1982 (with an average of 34 cases per month in 1981 and an average of 71 cases per month in 1982).

9. I do not have complete figures on how many of the complaints filed with the clerk were sent to mediation. The policy of sending complaints to mediation had only recently been instituted when my study began, but during some weeks my estimate is that one in three complaints went to mediation, while in others few were taken by the program.

10. See footnote 18, Chapter 4, p. 142.

11. Motor vehicle complaint hearings were scheduled every day from 9:00 to 11:00 A.M. Citizen hearings, scheduled only on certain weekdays, were given the remaining hour (and frequently less).

12. See discussion of bad check complaints in n.8.

13. Fourteen percent (120) of 882 complaints filed with the clerk during the 6-month period of my research were for nonsupport and welfare fraud, while 4% (34) involved code violations.

14. Wickersham Commission, 1931, p. 9; and see Chapter 2, pp. 27–28.

15. See Harrington, 1982.

16. For other examples of this reliance on technicalities by the Essex clerk, see Chapter 4, p. 57. For an example of how "technicality" can be transformed to a more substantive discussion of injury, see pp. 73–74.

17. Bourdieu, 1987, pp. 232–233.

18. See Harrington and Merry, 1988, p. 730.

19. See Chapter 4, note 19.

20. See note 8, above.

21. See Emerson, 1983, pp. 428–430.

22. Other differences in the flow of cases emerge from court policy that complaints brought by town police should also be aired in show cause hearings, at the clerk's discretion, in Franklin County, but not in Essex. Forty-six percent (324) of 699 complaints filed with the clerk in Franklin County between June 1 and December 31, 1982 were brought by police, and 39% (127) of these were given a show couse hearing. In Essex, by contrast, only 3% (27) of the 882 complaints brought to the clerk were brought by police. Both courts had approximately the same frequencies of non-support and welfare fraud complaints brought by the Department of Public Welfare [12% (82) of 699 complaints in Franklin County, 14% (120) of 882 complaints in Essex]. Non-support and welfare fraud, like bad check complaints, typically involve more routine issues of administration (e.g., arranging a schedule of payment), rather than issues of conflict management or the interpretation of crime.

23. Unlike Salem, where citizen complaints were defined as the territory of the most junior clerk in the office, in Greenfield responsibility for conducting complaint hearings was distributed relatively equally between the Clerk Magistrate and an Assistant Clerk. Of 507 hearings (including hearings that were observed and those recorded in court dockets) in which the identity of the clerk could be established, 234 were conducted by the Clerk Magistrate (Lawrence Simpson) and 273 by the Assistant Clerk Magistrate (Gabriel LeBlanc).

24. See discussion of complaint procedure, Chapter 4, pp. 53–56

25. This remark was made in reference to a series of cases in which the

same parties appeared repeatedly at the courthouse over a period of months. See discussion of these complaints in Chapter 6.

26. In my sample, 12 cases were related to runaway teenagers. All but 1 (brought by a runaway against her foster parents) were issued by the clerk.

27. In Massachusetts, the Clerk Magistrate is appointed by the governor, and the Assistant Clerk is appointed by the Clerk Magistrate (Massachusetts General Laws, chapter 218, sections 8, 10).

28. By implication, a "lower" class of people.

29. See also discussion of this complaint in Chapter 4, pp. 54–55.

30. See Chapter 2, pp. 18–19 for a discussion of continuances in Franklin County.

31. Bittner, 1969, p. 183.

32. Bourdieu, 1987, p. 224.

33. Bourdieu, 1977, p. 192,.discusses the concept of "gentle violence."

34. Bourdieu, 1987, p. 229.

35. Ibid., p. 225.

36. Butler, 1990, p. 15. Judith Butler uses this phrase in reference to what she describes as the "essential incompleteness" of the category "women."

Notes to Chapter 6

1. This phrase is commonly used by court staff to describe Turners Falls complainants.

2. Bourdieu, 1977, pp. 196, 171. And see discussion in Chapter 4, pp. 47–48.

3. de Certeau, 1984, p. 26, emphasis deleted.

4. See Comaroff and Comaroff (1987, pp. 191–194) for a discussion of a similar figure among the Tswana of South Africa.

5. My research assistant was warned by court staff towards the end of our research that Charlie was becoming more dangerous and that she should stay away from him.

6. For a related analysis, see Abu-Lughod's (1986, pp. 175–177) analysis of the emergence of meaning in Awlad 'Ali poetry in the context of what the audience knows about the performer. And see Holquist (1990, p. 157) for a discussion of the way meanings emerge in the tension between figure and ground (or plot and story) in Bakhtin's dialogism.

7. Greenhouse, 1988, p. 696. Greenhouse discusses a similar process in criminal court hearings in a Georgia town. See also the discussion of class hierarchies, and "the processes through which the low troubles the high" in Peter Stallybrass and Allon White, *The Politics and Poetics of Transgression*, p. 3.

8. Keller, "Man defends self on morals charge," *Greenfield Recorder*, May 17, 1983, p. 3; Keller, "Exam asked for man convicted on morals charges," *Greenfield Recorder*, May 18, 1983, p. 3; Keller, "Wertheimer sentenced to 7–10 years," *Greenfield Recorder*, May 27, 1983, p. 3.

9. Thus real cases: garbage cases:: criminal hearings: complaint hearings/rational people: irrational people/property offenses: relational quarrels/middle class rights: lower class nuisance. This hierarchy of distinctions recalls Mary Douglas' familiar discussion of the "elaborate cosmologies which pollution symbols reveal" (Douglas, 1966, p. 15); and see Bourdieu's argument about order

imposed through distinction (1977, p. 124). Bourdieu suggests further that "[s]ystems of classification which reproduce, in their own specific logic, the objective classes, i.e. the divisions by sex, age, or position in the relations of production, make their . . . contribution to the reproduction of power relations of which they are the product, by securing the misrecognition, and hence the recognition, of the arbitrariness on which they are based" (1977, p. 164). The social and political implications of Douglas' discussion of pollution are also developed in Peter Stalleybrass and Allon White's *The Politics and Poetics of Transgression*, which examines how the mapping of the social into high and low, polite and vulgar, constitutes the bourgeois subject by excluding the contaminating, repulsive and dirty (1986, p. 191).

10. See Greenhouse, 1992, for a discussion of the connections between restraint and cultural value in American society; and see Nader, 1990 for a more general discussion of the connections of an ideology of harmony to social control.

11. See discussion of response to this event in Greenfield, in Chapter 3, p. 37.

12. These rules require, for example, that families living in subsidized housing must provide separate rooms for different-sex children over 2 years of age. Some women I interviewed had been required to move repeatedly because of the age, or removal, of their children.

13. According to the 1980 census, the mean income of families in the downstreet neighborhood of Turners Falls was $14,549, 19% of 487 families had incomes below the poverty level, 9% of 644 people in the labor force were unemployed, and 22% of 747 income-receiving households received public assistance; 62% of the housing was occupied by renters, and 43% of the population was in multiple-family units; and 25% of 487 families living in the area were headed by single women (Center for Massachusetts Data, *Census of Population and Housing*, 1980, Summary area 16, STF 3 printout, Turners Falls: ED 32). (For data on a similar neighborhood in Greenfield, see Chapter 3, p. 41). By contrast, in a typical working-to-middle class neighborhood in Greenfield, the mean income was $19,532, 1.7% of 339 families had incomes below the poverty level, 5.2% of 595 people in the labor force were unemployed, and 10% of 492 income-receiving households received public assistance; 23% of the housing was occupied by renters, and 21% of the population was in multiple-family units; and 4% of 339 families were headed by single women (Center for Massachusetts Data, *Census of Population and Housing*, 1980, Summary Area 16, STF 3, Greenfield: ED 20).

14. *Greenfield Recorder*, April 5, 1983, p. 4.

15. *Greenfield Recorder*, December 19, 1983, p. 1.

16. *Greenfield Recorder*, September 7, 1982, pp. 1, 12.

17. *Greenfield Recorder*, April 29, 1983, p. 12, and September 7, 1982, p. 1.

18. *Greenfield Recorder*, November 11, 1982, p. 10.

19. Ibid., p. 10.

20. Greenfield Recorder, June 28, 1982, p. 10.

21. *Greenfield Recorder*, April 5, 1983, p. 3. The project developer, by contrast, said that "a dozen or so workers on the project were from Montague and surrounding towns," Greenfield Recorder, June 7, 1983, p. 3.

22. *Greenfield Recorder*, May 12, 1983, p. 3.

23. *Greenfield Recorder*, April 22, 1983, pp. 1, 12.

24. Ibid., p. 12.

25. *Greenfield Recorder*, May 12, 1983, p. 3.

26. The term "community" is used repeatedly in newspaper articles describing the transformation of Turners Falls. See, e.g. *Greenfield Recorder*, June 28, 1982, p. 1; November 11, 1982, p. 10; April 22, 1983, p. 1; April 29, 1983, p. 12; October 12, 1983, p. 1.

27. Retiring police sergeant from the Town of Montague, quoted in *Greenfield Recorder*, August 26, 1982, p. 1. (Turners Falls is one of 5 "villages" in Montague Township).

28. In the early 1970s, Michael Metallica's Renaissance Church was associated with alternative lifestyles, hippies, and an influx of "rich kids" from other parts of the country. Today, the commune is gone, although some of its abandoned property buildings stand near the Power Town complex.

29. In Greenfield, there were 25 neighborhood cases out of a total of 264 complaint applications fild with the clerk (1.4 per 1000 inhabitants). In Turners Falls, there were 26 neighborhood cases out of a total of 130 complaint applications filed. (The respective populations of the 2 towns are 18,436 for Greenfield and 4,711 for Turners Falls). These figures do not necessarily speak to "more" fighting in Turners Falls, but may instead reflect the general familiarity of Turners Falls residents with state agencies (including the court) and the ease with which they mobilize them to accomplish aims of their own.

30. de Certeau, 1984, p. 26; and see discussion above, pp.79–80.

31. The following discussion draws on docket data from all of the complaints, observations of 8 hearings, and interviews held with participants after the hearings. Portions of the discussion reproduce material from Yngvesson, 1988, pp. 435–440.

32. "Technical issuance" is discussed in Chapter 2, p. 18.

33. See Foucault, 1979, pp. 19-22.

34. The police subsequently described the knife as "a butter knife."

35. This was a common strategy for the head clerk in controversial cases, and meant that he would notify the parties of his decision in a few days.

36. Eco, 1979, p. 80.

37. Eco, (1979, pp. 79ff.) discusses the coexistence of superimposed semantic fields in contexts of cultural pluralism and the diverse possibilities open to a language user in these situations for coupling a particular "sign vehicle" with a particular meaning. He notes the rapidity with which a semantic field can disintegrate and restructure itself into a new field in these situations. See also Bourdieu's (1977, pp. 40, 170–171) discussion of the political significance of official "authorized" meanings and the objectification (legitimation) of particular versions of reality through the imposition of these.

38. Fantasia, 1988, p. 17.

39. Williams, 1977, p. 114.

Notes to Chapter 7

1. The Diggers (an offshoot of the Levelers) were Puritan extremists who advocated an egalitarian and communistic society based on common ownership of land. Their encroachment on the property of landowners was resisted and the community was eventually destroyed in 1650 by mob violence. See Winstanley, 1652, and Hill, 1972.

2. "The World Turned Upside Down," Rosselson, 1975.

3. Ibid.

4. See Chapter 5, p. 74.

5. Pocock, 1985, p. 104. Pocock sees these as two distinct traditions of property. One, deriving from Aristotle, involves property as "an extension and a prerequisite of personality"; in this tradition, property was the basis of civic virtue (viewed as the capacity for governance). In the second tradition, deriving from Rome and developed in the seventeenth century by philosopher John Locke, property does not lose its significance to personality, but is understood as well as "that to which you have a right." In this latter tradition property becomes "a system of legally defined relations between persons and things, or between persons through things."

6. See Constance Perin's discussion of home ownership as the American dream and "the ideal of perfected citizenship" (1977, p. 76, and more generally, pp. 32–80).

7. Center of Massachusetts Data, *Census of Population and Housing*, 1990, Summary Tape File 3, Town of Leverett, p. 1. In 1980, the population was 1471 (*Census of Population and Housing*, 1980, Summary Tape File 3, Town of Leverett, p. 1). According to figures provided at a 1989 Town Meeting in Leverett, the population of the town increased by 52% between 1970 and 1985. In the 20 previous years (1950–1970), population increased by 27%, while between 1910 and 1950 the town grew by only 8.7%.

8. The tax rate in Leverett doubled between 1975 and 1992, going from $7.00 per $100 of real estate property value to $15.

9. For example, by-laws regulating the development of rear lots, frontage requirements, requirements for site plan review, and for controlling erosion and protecting aquifers were introduced or modified in town meetings between 1987 and 1989 (Town of Leverett, Amendments to Zoning By-Laws, 1987–1989). In addition, the criteria for getting a special permit (for example, to allow a longer driveway than the 500 feet provided in the by-laws) were changed.

10. Town of Leverett, Zoning By-Laws, 1988, Article 11.

11. "The World Turned Upside Down," Rosselson, 1975.

12. Names have been changed. I did not interview Hudson and Garfield in constructing my account of this case. I began my research at the end of a long and emotionally draining court battle over their right to develop Long Hill, and was told by people who knew them that it would not be an appropriate time to speak with them about the controversy. As a result, my account focuses on the meaning of the conflict from the point of view of opponents to the development, although I also spoke with people who supported Hudson's and Garfield's position. Since my principal interest in this case is in the connections it reveals between rights to private property and the capacity to make legal arguments about "community" and about collective needs, interviews with opponents to the development (who focused on issues of collective needs) were more central for my analysis.

13. Town of Leverett, Zoning By-Laws, 1988, section VI.F(4).

14. Town of Leverett, Zoning By-Laws, 1988, section III.

15. The Echo Lake Association is a private association of landowners with property abutting the lake.

16. Town of Leverett, Board of Appeals, *Notice of Decision*, August 1, 1988. Lot #3 in Figure 7.1B was created in 1990, just before all three of the

building lots in Figure 7.1B were sold to abutters. At the time of Hudson's request for a variance, what became lot #3 was the frontage to her rear lot of 24 acres (this lot was subsequently reduced to 19 acres when lot #3 was created, landlocking the 19 acre parcel).

17. Town of Leverett, Board of Appeals, Report of Finding, August 1, 1988,pp. 1 and 3 (emphasis added).

18. A perk test in the area where Hudson's house would have to be built (if a variance could not be obtained from the Zoning Board for a driveway from Camp Road) did not meet required standards.

19. Town of Leverett, Board of Appeals, *Decision* and *Report of Finding*, July 12, 1989.

20. Because the legal residence of summer home owners is elsewhere, they do not vote in Leverett, and thus do not come to Town Meeting. Some do not get mail in Leverett, and thus do not receive the newsletter.

21. See Chapter 3, pp. 43–44.

22. See discussion of governance by the clerks in Chapters 4 and 5.

23. Complaint for Judicial Review filed with the Massachusetts Trial Court, Superior Court Department, Franklin Division, July 27, 1989, p. 4.

24. "The World Turned Upside Down," Rosselson, 1975.

25. *Greenfield Recorder*, May 3, 1991, p. 9.

26. "Hill Top Development in Leverett," 1989, pp. 1 and 3; letter to ZBA from Long View Alliance, 1989.

27. See above, p. 100.

28. The three conditions that must be met in order to grant a variance are (1) that the problem confronting the applicant must arise from "circumstances relating to the soil conditions, shape, or topography of the land"; (2) that literal enforcement of the By-Law must involve "substantial hardship, financial or otherwise" to the applicant; and (3) that the variance would not "substantially derogate from the intent of the By-Law" (Massachusetts General Laws, chapter 40A, section 10).

29. See Yngvesson, 1988, p. 428 and Perin, 1977, pp. 105–106.

30. "The World Turned Upside Down," Rosselson, 1975.

31. Ibid.

32. Commonwealth of Massachusetts, Franklin, SS., Superior Court Civil Action No. 89–118, *Memorandum of Decision and Order on Plaintiffs Motion for Summary Judgment.*

33. *Amherst Bulletin*, November 7, 1990, p. 1, section 2.

34. *Daily Hampshire Gazette*, November 8, 1990; other articles reporting the victory in court appeared in the *Amherst Bulletin*, November 7, 1990 and in the *Springfield Sunday Republican*, November 11, 1990;.

35. *Daily Hampshire Gazette*, April 6, 1991, p. 9; *Amherst Bulletin*, April 6, 1991, p. 9; *Amherst Bulletin*, April 10, 1991, p. 9.

36. *Daily Hampshire Gazette*, April 6, 1991, p. 9.

37. Bourdieu, 1977, p. 179.

38. Ibid., p. 192.

39. Ibid., p. 191.

40. Some months after the purchase, a tag sale was organized by residents who had not previously been involved in the lawsuit or the purchase, in order to help raise funds to defray costs of the purchase. A year later, a spinoff group from the Alliance had formed to control algae growth in Echo Lake.

Notes to Chapter 8

1. Engel, 1984; Merry and Silbey, 1984; Baumgartner, 1985; Greenhouse, 1986; Ellickson, 1991.

2. Crolius, *Amherst Bulletin*, September 13, 1989, p. 5.

3. Pocock, 1985, p. 104. Pocock defines propriety as "that which pertained or was proper to a person or situation."

4. Ibid., p. 48.

5. See discussion of Justice Brandeis' celebrated dissent to *Olmstead v. United States* (1928) in White, 1990, pp. 149–154. Brandeis' dissent defined "the right to be let alone" as "the most comprehensive of rights and the right most valued by civilized men" (White, 1990, p. 154, citing Brandeis).

6. Tocqueville, 1850 (1969), p. 270.

7. Abu-Lughod, 1990, p. 52.

8. Foucault, 1982, p. 223.

9. Bourdieu, 1977, p. 196.

10. Williams, 1977, p. 114.

11. Mitchell, 1990, p. 561.

12. See, in this connection, Marcus and Fischer's discussion of the appropriation of "the rubbish available within a preconstituted market" by working-class and ethnic communities, as a dimension of what they term "society-wide struggles for defining authoritative and other possible meanings of events for a diverse public." They note that these appropriations may be simply "expressions of reality," or that they may be interpreted as "contestatory political mobilizations against 'the system'" (1986, p. 153).

13. Donzelot, 1979.

14. de Certeau, 1984, p. 179.

15. Bourdieu, 1977, p. 179.

16. See discussion of the "assault with a pumpkin" in Chapter 4, and of the last hearing in "A Bad Neighborhood," in Chapter 6.

17. de Certeau, 1984, p. 18.

18. Tocqueville, 1969, p. 248.

19. Abu-Lughod, 1990, p. 52.

20. de Certeau, 1984, p. 26.

21. Scott (1985) suggests that resistance is enabled by a sphere of consciousness that is "outside" power relations. For a critique of Scott's position, see Mitchell, 1990.

22. Comaroff and Comaroff, 1991, p. 26; Genovese, 1974; Kaplan, 1990.

23. From an interview of Jamaica Kincaid by Donna Perry (Perry, 1990, p. 507).

24. Kincaid, 1990, p. 18.

25. Perry, 1990, p. 508.

26. Clifford, 1988, p. 344.

27. Ibid., p. 342.

28. Ibid., p. 344.

29. Bourdieu, 1977, p. 196.

30. Winnicott, 1982, p. 103.

31. Bourdieu, 1977, p. 79. Bourdieu's analysis of invention here relates the "buried possibility" back to structures which are both the product and source of practices; "discourse continually feeds off itself like a train bringing along its own rails" (79). I am arguing for a more radical possibility in the blurring

of self and other as a psychological process that does not (or need not) always merely reproduce established categories and distinctions (Winnicott 1982; Mahoney and Yngvesson 1992, p. 21). Bakhtin's discussion of historical poetics as the way "given" (transhistorical) narrative forms are interpreted at a particular historical moment, freeing these forms from the circumscribed meanings of another time and place, is also relevant here (Holquist, 1990, pp. 111–118; and see Bakhtin, 1981). I interpret the innovative use of imagery about the Diggers by the Long View Alliance and the creative use of cultural imagery by Charlie, or by the Assistant Clerk, in this way. In a similar way, Bakhtin argues that the self is not confined to the values through which it is realized at a particular point in time, but that in other times, "there will always be other configurations of [self/other] . . . relations, and in conjunction with that other, my self will be differently understood" (Holquist, 1990, p. 38).

32. Baudrillard, 1988, p. 91.

APPENDIX

Appendix 1: Complaints Applications Filed with the Court Clerk in Franklin County, June 1–December 31, 1982*

Complaint Type	Frequency	Percent
A&B (assault & battery)	135	21.4
A&B, dangerous weapon	7	1.1
Assault	8	1.3
Assault—intent murder	1	0.2
Assault—dangerous weapon	7	1.1
Malicious destruction	24	3.8
Wanton destruction	25	4.0
Break glass bldg	1	0.2
B&E (breaking and entering)	3	0.5
B&E (night)	10	1.6
B&E (day)	12	1.9
B&E (night, intent misdemeanor)	5	0.8
B&E (night, intent felony)	18	2.9
B&E (day, intent misdemeanor)	2	0.3
B&E (day, intent felony)	19	3.0
Larceny over $100	46	7.3
Larceny under $100	33	5.2
Larceny in bldg	2	0.3
Larceny of motor vehicle (MV)	12	1.9
Unauthorized use of MV	2	0.3
Larceny by check	27	4.3
Forgery	7	1.1
Uttering	1	0.2
Rcvg stolen property	13	2.1
Shoplifting	6	1.0
Threat commit crime	8	1.3
Threat commit crime	2	0.3
Annoying phone calls	8	1.3
Obscene phone calls	2	0.3
Annoying, threatening phonecalls	5	0.8
Open gross lewdness	4	0.6
Indecent exposure	3	0.5
Accosting	2	0.3
Disorderly conduct	7	1.1
Disturbing peace	11	1.7
Violation 209A	2	0.3
Trespassing	22	3.5
Kidnapping	1	0.2

Complaint Type	Frequency	Percent
Custodial interference	3	0.5
Possession marijuana	12	1.9
Distribution marijuana	1	0.2
Possession other	2	0.3
Distribution other	1	0.2
Minor with alcohol	13	2.1
Procure alcohol	9	1.4
Contributing delinquency of minor	6	1.0
Nonsupport	2	0.3
False MV registration	1	0.2
False state MV theft	1	0.2
Fugitive	6	1.0
Failure appear	3	0.5
Witness intimidation	2	0.3
Health violation	2	0.3
Lessor/landlord	2	0.3
Failure pay wages	1	0.2
Discharge firearm	3	0.5
False fire alarm	3	0.5
By-Laws violation	1	0.2
Leash law	3	0.5
Solicitation without permit	3	0.5
Removing loam	1	0.2
Cutting wood	1	0.2
Destruction tree	1	0.2
Business Sunday	2	0.3
Trash on highway	2	0.3
Break glass road	2	0.3
Fishing hatchery	1	0.2
Ride locomotive	1	0.2
Hit dog with car	1	0.2
Rape	8	1.3
Miscellaneous other	14	2.6
Total	617	100.0

* This appendix provides additional detail on complaints discussed in Chapter 2. It does not include applications for non-support and for welfare fraud filed by the Department of Public Welfare.

Appendix 2: Owners vs Renters[a]

Neighborhood A (mean income $13,603)

Persons in occupied units by tenure

Total	584	
Renter occupied	398	(68%)

Multiple versus single-family units

Total	584	
Single	134	(23%)
Multiple	450	(77%)

Family households by presence of own children by family type

	With own children	Without own children	Total	
Married couple family	30	74	104	(59%)
Female householder, no husband present	52	21	73	(41%)
Total	82	95	177	(100%)

Neighborhood B (mean income $23,161)

Persons in occupied units by tenure

Total	1581	
Renter occupied	355	(22%)

Multiple versus single-family units

Total	1581	
Single	1347	(85%)
Multiple	234	(15%)

Family households by presence of own children by family type

	With own children	Without own children	Total	
Married couple family	143	187	330	(88%)
Female householder, no husband present	41	6	47	(12%)
Total	184	193	377	(100%)

a. Data are taken from the 1980 *Census of Population and Housing*, Summary Level 16, Greenfield, ED 0018 (pp. 2 and 9)and ED 0021U (pp. 2 and 9).

BIBLIOGRAPHY

Abel, Richard L. 1982. "The Contradictions of Informal Justice." In Richard L. Abel (ed.), *The Politics of Informal Justice*, Vol. I. New York: Academic Press.

Abu-Lughod, Lila. 1990. "The Romance of Resistance." *American Ethnologist*, 17(1):41–55.

Administrative Office of the District Court Department. 1975. *Standards of Judicial Practice*. "The Complaint Procedure." The Committee on Standards, Boston: District Court of Massachusetts.

———. 1982. *Report on Court Statistics for Fiscal Year 1982.*

———. 1984. "Elimination of the Trial de Novo System in Criminal Cases." *Report of the Committee of Juries of Six.*

American Bar Association. 1909. "Report of the Special Committee to Suggest Remedies and Formulate Proposed Laws to Prevent Delay and Unnecessary Cost in Litigation." *American Bar Association Journal*, 34:578

Amherst Bulletin. 1990. "ZBA variance for Long Hill access is struck down." November 7:1(sec. 2).

———. 1991. "Neighbors attempt to purchase hilltop by Leverett Pond." April 6:9; "Neighbors seeking grants to assist Long Hill purchase." April 9:9.

Atkinson, J. Maxwell, and Paul Drew. 1979. *Order in Court: The Organization of Verbal Interaction in Judicial Settings*. Atlantic Highlands, NJ: Humanities Press.

Aubert, Vilhelm. 1963. "Researches in the Sociology of Law." *The American Behavioral Scientist*, 7(9):16–20.

Auerbach, Jerold S. 1983. *Justice Without Trial? Resolving Disputes Without Lawyers*. New York: Oxford University Press.

Bailey, F. G. 1960. *Tribe, Caste and Nation*. Manchester: Manchester University Press.

Bakhtin, Mikhail M. 1981. "Forms of Time and of Chronotope in the Novel." In Michael Holquist (ed.), *The Dialogic Imagination: Four Essays by M.M. Bakhtin*, Austin, TX: University of Texas Press.

Banton, Michael. 1964. *The Policeman in the Community*. New York: Basic Books.

Barth, Frederick, 1966. *Models of Social Organization*. No. 23, Occasional Papers of the Royal Anthropological Institute.

Baudrillard, Jean. 1988. *Selected Writings*. Mark Poster (ed.). Oxford: Polity Press.

Baumgartner, Mary Pat. 1985. "Law and the Middle Class: Evidence from a Suburban Town." *Law and Human Behavior*, 9:3–24

Bender, Thomas. 1978. *Community and Social Change in America*. Baltimore: Johns Hopkins.

Bittner, Egon, 1969. "The Police on Skid Row." In Richard Quinney (ed.), *Crime and Justice in Society*. Boston: Little, Brown.

———. 1974. "Florence Nightingale in Pursuit of Willie Sutton: A Theory of the Police." In Herbert Jacob (ed.), *The Potential for Reform of Criminal Justice*. Beverly Hills, CA: Sage.

Black, Barbara. 1980. "Community and Law in Seventeenth-Century Massachusetts." *Yale Law Journal*, 90:232–246.

Bourdieu, Pierre. 1977. *Outline of a Theory of Practice*. Cambridge: Cambridge University Press.

———. 1987. "The Force of Law." *The Hastings Law Journal*, 38:201–248.

Botein, Stephen, 1981. "The Legal Profession in Colonial North America." In Wilfrid Priest (ed.), *Lawyers in Early Modern Europe and America*. New York: Holmes and Meier.

Boyer, Paul, and Stephen Nissenbaum, 1974. *Salem Possessed: The Social Origins of Witchcraft*. Cambridge: Harvard University Press.

Brigham, John, 1988. "The Bias of Constitutional Property: Toward Compensation for the Elimination of Statutory Entitlements." *Law and Inequality: A Journal of Theory and Inequality*, 5:405–429.

Bruner, Jerome (ed.). 1984. *Text, Play, and Story: The Construction and Reconstruction of Self and Society*. Prospect Heights, IL: Waveland Press.

Butler, Judith. 1990. *Gender Trouble*. New York: Routledge.

Cain, Maureen, and Kalman Kulcsar. 1981–1982. "Thinking Disputes: An Essay on the Origins of the Dispute Industry." *Law and Society Review*, 16(3):375–402.

Carroll, David. 1987. "Narrative, Heterogeneity, and the Question of the Political: Bakhtin and Lyotard." In Murray Krieger (ed.), *The Aims of Representation: Subject/Text/History*. New York: Columbia University Press.

Center for Massachusetts Data. 1980. *Census of Population and Housing*.

———. 1990. *Census of Population and Housing*.

Clifford, James. 1988. *The Predicament of Culture: Twentieth-Century Ethnography, Literature, and Art*. Cambridge: Harvard University Press.

Collier, Jane F. 1973. *Law and Social Change in Zinacantan*. Stanford: Stanford University Press.

Collier, Jane F., Michelle Rosaldo, and Sylvia Yanagisako. 1982. "Is There a Family?" In Barrie Thorne and Marilyn Yalom (eds.), *Rethinking the Family: Some Feminist Questions*. New York: Longman.

Colson, Elizabeth. 1953. "Social Control and Vengeance in Plateau Tonga Society." *Africa*, 23:199–212.

Comaroff, John L., and Simon Roberts. 1981. *Rules and Processes*. Chicago: University of Chicago Press.

Comaroff, John L., and Jean Comaroff. 1991. *Of Revelation and Revolution: Christianity, Colonialism, and Consciousness in South Africa*, Vol. 1. Chicago: University Press.

County Commissioners. 1981–1982. *County, State and Town Officers for Franklin County, Massachusetts*.

Cowin, Judith A. 1978. "Court Reorganization and the District Courts." *Massachusetts Law Review*. 63(5):191–193.

Crolius, Ali. 1989. "Public Good Should Supersede Developer's Rights." *Amherst Bulletin*, September 13:5.

Daily Hampshire Gazette. 1990. "Leverett alliance blocks road." November 8:9.
————. 1991. "Residents rally 'round a hilltop." April 6:9.
Danzig, Richard, 1973. "Toward the Creation of a Complementary, Decentralized System of Criminal Justice." *Stanford Law Review*, 26:1–54.
Danzig, Richard, and Michael J. Lowy. 1975. "Everyday Disputes and Mediation in the United States: A Reply to Professor Fetsliner." *Law and Society Review*, 9:675–694.
Davis, Natalie Z. 1987. *Fiction in the Archives.* Stanford: Stanford University Press.
de Certeau, Michel. 1984. *The Practice of Everyday Life.* Berkeley: University of California Press.
Donzelot, J. 1979. *The Policing of Families.* New York: Pantheon.
Douglas, Mary, 1966. *Purity and Danger: An Analysis of Concepts of Pollution and Taboo.* Harmondsworth, England: Penguin.
Eckhoff, Torstein, 1966. "The Mediator and the Judge." *Acta Sociologica*, 10:158–166.
Eco, Umberto. 1979. *A Theory of Semiotics.* Bloomington:University of Indiana Press.
Eisenstein, James and Herbert Jacob. 1977. *Felony Justice: An Organizational Analysis of Criminal Courts.* Boston: Little, Brown.
Ellickson, Robert C. 1991. *Order Without Law: How Neighbors Settle Disputes.* Cambridge: Harvard University Press.
Ellis, Richard E. 1971. *The Jeffersonian Crisis: Courts and Politics in the Young Republic.* New York: Oxford University Press.
Emerson, Robert M. 1969. *Judging Delinquents: Context and Process in Juvenile Court.* Chicago: Aldine.
————.1983. "Holistic Effects in Social Control Decision-making." *Law and Society Review.* 17:425–456.
Emerson, Robert, and Sheldon Messinger. 1977. "The Micro-Politics of Trouble." *Social Problems*, 25(2):121–134.
Engel, David M. 1984. "The Oven Bird's Song: Insiders, Outsiders, and Personal Injuries in an American Community." *Law and Society Review*, 18(4):551–582.
————. 1987. "Law, Time, and Community." *Law and Society Review.* 21(4):605–638.
Epstein, A.L. (ed.).1967. *The Craft of Social Anthropology.* London: Tavistock.
Fantasia, Rick. 1988. *Cultures of Solidarity: Consciousness, Action and Contemporary American Workers.* Berkeley: University of California Press.
Feeley, Malcolm M. (ed.). 1979. *Plea Bargaining.* Special Issue, *Law and Society Review.* 13(2).
Felstiner, William L.F., Richard L. Abel, and Austin Sarat. 1980–1981. "The Emergence and Transformation of Disputes: Naming, Blaming, Claiming." *Law and Society Review*, 15(3–4):631–654.
Fitzpatrick, Peter, 1988. "The Rise and Rise of Informalism." In Roger Matthews (ed.), *Informal Justice?* London: Sage.
Foucault, Michel. 1979. *Discipline and Punish: The Birth of the Prison.* New York: Vintage.
————.1980. *The History of Sexuality*, Vol.I, New York: Random House.

————.1982. "The Subject and Power," In Hubert L. Dreyfus and Paul Rabinow (eds.), *Michel Foucault: Beyond Structuralism and Hermeneutics*. Chicago: University of Chicago Press.

Gawalt, Gerard W. 1970. "Sources of Anti-Lawyer Sentiment in Massachusetts, 1740–1840." *American Journal of Legal History*, 14:283–307.

Geertz, Clifford. 1973. *The Interpretation of Cultures*. New York: Basic Books.

Genovese, Eugene D. 1974. *Roll, Jordan, Roll: The World the Slaves Made*, New York: Pantheon.

Giddens, Anthony. 1979. *Central Problems in Social Theory: Action, Structure and Contradiction in Social Analysis*. University of California Press.

Ginsburg, Faye. 1989. *Contested Lives: The Abortion Debate in an American Community*. Berkeley: University of California Press.

Goebel, Julius, Jr., and T. Raymond Naughton. 1944. *Law Enforcement in Colonial New York*. New York: The Commonwealth Fund.

Gordon, Linda. 1988. *Heroes of Their Own Lives*. New York: Viking Penguin.

Greenberg, Douglas. 1976. *Crime and Law Enforcement in the Colony of New York, 1691–1776*. Ithaca: Cornell University Press.

Greenfield Recorder. 1982. "Candidates support override: Blackbird, Oberg agree on most issues." March 23:1; "New historic district can boost Judd project." June 28:1; "More data sought on mall plan." July 2:3; "Video games plan opposed." July 16:1; "Builder predicts Turners revival." September 7:1,12; "Unemployment blues on rise." November 6:1,10; "Reviving Turners: Editorial." November 11:10; "Machinists' future uncertain." November 19:14; "Counties to fight registry takeover." December 29:12.

————. 1983 " GTD looks at future." January 24:1; "Charter reform needs a big push: Editorial." February 8:8; "WMass. counties face challenge of change." February 15:1; "County and commonwealth: Strained relations at best." February 17:16; "Counties' future tied to legislative action." February 18:10; "Protest : GTD workers oppose wage, benefits rollback." March 31:1; "Hiring practices at Turners housing project criticized." April 5:4; "Turners housing project developer counters rumors." April 22:1,12; "Think positive in Turners: Editorial." April 29:12; "GTD workers start strike." May 3:1; "GTD strike vote given much thought." May 11:9; "Developers promise to be good neighbors." May 12:3; "Without homes, families, singles look out for shelter." May 18:1; "Project's labor discussed." June 7:3; "UE–GTD talks cancelled after 3 arrests." June 25:3; "Miles Street: Merchants band together to fight street's troubled image." July 29:12; "Town has much to lose in GTD strike: Editorial."August 11:12; "Feeling good about downtown revitalization: Editorial." August 15:10; "GTD strike over; union ratifies pact." August 25:1; "After 29 years as police officer, John Zebrowski's going fishin'." August 26:1.16; "Poor management caused cutting-tool industry's woes." October 8:1; "Ave. A facelift designers 'go for it'." October 12:1; "State official urges toolmakers to find new uses for plants." October 15:3; "Turners housing dedicated." December 19:1.

————. 1991. "Offended by action." May 3:9.

Greenhouse, Carol J. 1982. "Looking at Culture, Looking for Rules." *Man*, 17:58–73.

———. 1986. *Praying for Justice: Faith, Order and Community in an American Town*. Ithaca: Cornell University Press.

———. 1988. "Courting Difference: Issues of Interpretation and Comparison in the Study of Legal Ideologies." *Law and Society Review*. 88(4):687–708.

———. 1991. "Reading Violence." Paper presented at Amherst College Colloquium, *Law and Violence*, Spring.

———. 1992. "Signs of Quality: Individualism and Hierarchy in American Culture." *American Ethnologist*, 19(2):233–254.

Greenhouse, Carol J. et al. 1993. *Contest and Community: The Meanings of Law in Three American Towns*.

Gulliver, Philip H. 1963. *Social Control in an African Society*. Boston University Press.

Harley, Herbert. 1915. "Court Organization for a Metropolitan District." *American Political Science Review*, 9:507–518.

Harrington, Christine B. 1982. "Delegalization Reform Movements: A Historical Analysis." In Richard Abel (ed.), *The Politics of Informal Justice*, Vol.1. New York: Academic Press.

———. 1985. *Shadow Justice: The Ideology and Institutionalization of Alternatives to Court*. Westport, CN: Greenwood Press.

Harrington, Christine B., and Sally E. Merry, 1988. "Ideological Production: The Making of Community Mediation." *Law and Society Review*. 22(4):709–736.

Hartog, Hendrik. 1976. "The Public Law of a County Court; Judicial Government in Eighteenth Century Massachusetts." *American Journal of Legal History*, 20:282–329.

———. 1990. "Abigail Bailey's Couverture: Law in a Married Woman's Consciousness." Unpublished Manuscript. Madison: University of Wisconsin.

Haskins, George L. 1960. *Law and Authority in Early Massachusetts: A Study in Tradition and Design*. New York: Macmillan.

———. 1984. "Lay Judges: Magistrates and Justices in Early Massachusetts." In *Law in Colonial Massachusetts (1630–1800)*. Boston: The Colonial Society of Massachusetts.

Heilbrun, Carolyn G. 1988. *Writing a Woman's Life*. New York: Norton.

Hill, Christopher. 1972. *The World Turned Upside Down: Radical Ideas During the English Revolution*. New York: Penguin.

Hoebel, E. Adamson. 1954. *The Law of Primitive Man: A Study in Comparative Legal Dynamics*. Cambridge: Harvard University Press.

Holquist, Michael. 1990. *Dialogism: Bakhtin and His World*. New York: Routledge.

Horowitz, Morton. 1977. *The Transformation of American Law, 1780–1860*. Cambridge: Harvard University Press.

Jenkins, Paul. 1982. *The Conservative Rebel: A Social History of Greenfield Massachusetts*. Greenfield, MA: Town of Greenfield.

Jones, Douglas L. 1984. "The Transformation of the Law of Poverty in Eighteenth-Century Massachusetts." In *Law in Colonial Massachusetts, 1630–1800*. Boston: The Colonial Society of Massachusetts.

Kaplan, Martha, 1990. "Meaning, Agency, and Colonial History:

Navosavakadna and the Tuka Movement in Fiji." *American Ethnologist*, 17(1):3–22.

Keebler, Robert S. 1930. "Our Justice of the Peace Courts—A Problem in Justice," *Tennessee Law Review*. 9:1–21.

Keller, Charles. 1983a. "Man defends self on morals charge." *Greenfield Recorder*, May 17:3.

———. 1983b. "Exam asked for man convicted on morals charges." *Greenfield Recorder*, May 18:3.

———. 1983c. "Wertheimer sentenced to 7–10 years." *Greenfield Recorder*, May 27:3.

Kincaid, Jamaica. 1990. *Lucy*. New York: Farrar Straus Giroux.

Konig, David T. 1979. *Law and Society in Puritan Massachusetts: Essex County, 1629–1692*. Chapel Hill: University of North Carolina Press.

Lane, Roger. 1967. *Policing the City: Boston, 1822–1885*. Boston: Harvard Universtiy Press.

Legal Studies Forum. 1985. *Special Issue on Law, Ideology and Social Research*, IX(1).

Lukes, Stephen. 1974. *Power: A Radical View*. London: Macmillan.

Maguire, John M. 1926. "The Model Poor Litigants' Statute." *Annals of the American Academy of Political and Social Science*, 125:84–90.

Mahoney, Maureen A. and Barbara Yngvesson. 1992. "The Construction of Subjectivity and the Paradox of Resistance: Reintegrating Feminist Anthropology and Psychology." *Signs*, 18(1):44–73.

Marcus, George E. and Michael M.J. Fischer. 1986. *Anthropology as Cultural Critique: An Experimental Moment in the Human Sciences*. Chicago: Chicago University Press.

Massachusetts General Laws. chapter 218, section 35A.

———. chapter 40A, section 10.

Mather, Lynn. 1974. "The Outsider in the Courtroom: An Alternative Role for the Defense." In Herbert Jacob (ed.) *The Potential for Reform of Criminal Justice*. Beverly Hills, CA: Sage.

———. 1979. *Plea-Bargaining or Trial? The Process of Criminal-Case Disposition*. Lexington, MA: D. C. Heath.

Mather, Lynn, and Barbara Yngvesson. 1980–1981. "Language, Audience, and the Transformation of Disputes." *Law and Society Review*, 15:755–821.

Maynard, Douglas W. 1988. "Narratives and Narrative Structure in Plea Bargaining." *Law and Society Review*. 22(3):449–482.

McBarnet, Doreen. 1981. "Magistrates' Courts and the Ideology of Justice." *British Journal of Law and Society*, 8:181–197.

McDermott, Kathleen, 1983. "The Development of the District Courts of the Commonwealth of Massachusetts; 1821 to 1920. Unpublished paper. Northampton, MA.

Merry, Sally E. 1981. "The Social Organization of Mediation in Non-Industrial Societies: Implications for Informal Justice in America." In Richard Abel (ed.), *Informal Justice*. New York: Academic Press.

———. 1982. "Defining 'Success' in the Neighborhood Justice Movement." In Roman Tomasic and Malcolm M. Feeley (eds.), *Neighborhood Justice: Assessment of an Emerging Idea*. New York: Langman.

———. 1987. "Disputing Without Culture: Review Essay of Dispute Resolution." *Harvard Law Review*, 100:2057–2073.

————. 1990. *Getting Justice and Getting Even: The Legal Consciousness of Working Class Americans.* Chicago: University of Chicago Press.

Merry, Sally E., and Susan S. Silbey. 1984. "What Do Plaintiffs Want? Reexamining the Concept of Dispute." *The Justice System Journal,* 9(2):151–178.

Mitchell, Timothy. 1990. "Everyday Metaphors of Power." *Theory and Society,* 19:545–577.

Moore, Sally F 1972. "Legal Liability and Evolutionary Interpretation: Some Aspects of Strict Liability, Self-Help and Collective Responsibility." In Max Gluckman (ed.), *The Allocation of Responsibility.* Manchester: The University Press.

————. 1977. "Individual Interests and Organizational Structures: Dispute Settlements as Events of Articulation." In Ian Hamnett (ed.), *Social Anthropology and Law.* New York: Academic Press.

————. 1982. "Law and Social Change: The Semi-Autonomous Social Field as an Appropriate Subject of Study." In Sally F. Moore, *Law as Process: An Anthropological Approach.* London: Routledge and Kegan Paul.

Morgan, Edmund S. (ed.) 1965. *Puritan Political Ideas, 1558–1794.* Indianapolis: Bobbs-Merrill.

Nader, Laura. 1965. "The Anthropological Study of Law." *American Anthropologist,* 67(6):3–32

————. 1969. *Law in Culture and Society.* Chicago: Aldine.

————. 1990. *Harmony Ideology: Justice and Control in a Zapotec Mountain Village.* Stanford: Stanford University Press.

Nader, Laura, and Harry L. Todd. 1978. *The Disputing Process: Law in Ten Societies.* New York: Columbia University Press.

Nelson, William E. 1981. *Dispute and Conflict Resolution in Plymouth County, Massachusetts, 1725–1825.* Chapel Hill: University of North Carolina Press

New York Times. 1989. "4 Slayings in 2 Years End Town's Century Without Any Killing." May 18:B10.

————. 1991. "Five Massachusetts Towns Continue a Tradition of Rebellions." May 19:14.

O'Barr, William M., and John M. Conley. 1985. "Litigant Satisfaction versus Legal Adequacy in Small Claims Court Narratives." *Law and Society Review,* 19(4):661–702.

Olmstead v. United States. 1928. 277 U.S. 438.

Ortner, Sherry. 1984. "Theory in Anthropology Since the Sixties." *Comparative Studies in Society and History,* 26(1):126–166.

Perin, Constance, 1977. *Everything in Its Place: Social Order and Land Use in America.* Princeton: Princeton University Press.

Perry, Donna. 1990. "An Interview with Jamaica Kincaid." In Henry Louis Gates, Jr. (ed.), *Reading Black, Reading Feminist: A Critical Anthology.* New York: Meridian.

Phillips, Adam. 1988. *Winnicott.* Cambridge: Harvard University Press.

Platt, Anthony M. 1969. *The Child Savers: The Invention of Delinquency.* Chicago: University of Chicago Press.

Pocock, J. G. A. 1985. *Virtue, Commerce, and History.* Cambridge: Cambridge University Press.

President's Commission on Law Enforcement and Administration of Criminal

Justice. 1967. "The Lower Courts." In *The Challenge of Crime in a Free Society*, pp. 128–130. Reprinted in John A. Robertson (ed.), *Rough Justice: Perspectives on Lower Criminal Courts*. Boston: Little, Brown, 1974.

Provine, Doris Marie, 1986. *Judging Credentials: Nonlawyer Judges and the Politics of Professionalism*. Chicago: University of Chicago Press.

Rosselson, Leon. 1975. "The World Turned Upside Down" (The Diggers Song). In Peter Blood-Patterson (ed.), *Rise Up Singing*. Bethlehem, PA: Sing Out Corp. (1988).

Ryan, John Paul. 1980–1981. "Adjudication and Sentencing in a Misdemeanor Court: The Outcome Is the Punishment." *Law and Society Review*, 15(1):79–108.

Santos, Boaventura de Sousa. 1977. "The Law of the Oppressed: The Construction and Reproduction of Legality in Pasargada." *Law and Society Review*, 12(1):5–126.

———. 1987. "Law: A Map of Misreading. Toward a Postmodern Conception of Law." *Journal of Law and Society*, 14(3):279–302.

Sarat, Austin, and W.L.F. Felstiner. 1986. "Law and Strategy in the Divorce Lawyer's Office," *Law and Society Review*, 20(1):93–134.

Scott, Austin W. 1923. "Small Causes and Poor Litigants." *American Bar Association Journal*, 9:457–459.

Scott, James C. 1985. *Weapons of the Weak: Everyday Forms of Peasant Resistance*. New Haven: Yale University Press.

Shurtleff, N.B. (ed.) 1853–1854. *Records of the Governor and Company of the Massachusetts Bay in New England*. Boston: Mass. Records.

Smith, Chester. 1927. "The Justice of the Peace System in the United States." *California Law Review*, 15:118–141.

Smith, Joseph H. (ed.) 1961. *Colonial Justice in Western Massachusetts (1639–1702): The Pynchon Court Record*. Cambridge: Harvard University Press.

Smith, Reginald Heber, 1919. "Denial of Justice." *Journal of the American Judicature Society*, 4:112–121.

Snell, Ronald K. 1970. *The County Magistracy in Eighteenth-Century Massachusetts: 1692–1750*. Unpublished Ph.D. Dissertation, Princeton University.

Snyder, Francis G. 1981. "Anthropology, Dispute Processes and Law: A Critical Introduction." *British Journal of Law and Society*, 8(2):141–179.

Springfield Sunday Republican. 1990. "Judge overturns driveway variance." November 11:14F.

Stalleybrass, Peter, and Allon White. 1986. *The Politics and Poetics of Transgression*. Ithaca: Cornell University Press.

Starkey, Marion L. 1955. *A Little Rebellion*. New York: Knopf.

Starr, June. 1978. *Dispute and Settlement in Rural Turkey: An Ethnography of Law*. Leiden: E.J. Brill.

Starr, June, and Barbara Yngvesson. 1975. "Scarcity and Disputing: Zeroing-in on Compromise Decisions." *American Ethnologist*, 2(3):553–566.

Steedman, Carolyn L. 1987. *Landscape for a Good Woman*. New Brunswick, NJ: Rutgers University Press.

Steinberg, Allen. 1984. "From Private Prosecution to Plea Bargaining:

Criminal Prosecution, the District Attorney, and American Legal History." *Crime and Delinquency*, 30(4):568–592.

―――. 1989. "Criminal Prosecution, Assault and the Decriminalization of Everyday Life in Nineteenth Century Philadelphia." Unpublished paper. Presented at the Annual Meeting of the Law and Society Association, Madison, Wisconsin.

Stone, Deborah A. 1988. *Policy Paradox and Political Reason*. Boston: Scott, Foresman.

Sudnow, David. 1965. "Normal Crimes: Sociological Features of the Penal Code in a Public Defender Office." *Social Problems*, 12:255–270.

Swartz, Marc J., Victor W. Turner, and Arthur Tuden (eds.). 1966. *Political Anthropology*. Chicago: Aldine.

Taylor, Robert J. 1954. *Western Massachusetts in the Revolution*. Providence: Brown University Press.

Terdiman, Richard. 1985. *Discourse/Counter-Discourse*. Ithaca: Cornell University Press.

Tocqueville, Alexis de. 1850 (1969). *Democracy in America*, Vol. I Garden City, NY: Doubleday.

Town of Greenfield. 1895. Selectmen's *Annual Report* to the Town of Greenfield.

Town of Leverett. 1987–1989. *Zoning Bylaws*.

―――. 1988. Board of Appeals, *Decision and Report of Finding*, August 1, 1988.

―――. 1989. Board of Appeals, *Decision and Report of Finding*, July 12, 1989.

Tumey v. Ohio. 1927. 273 U.S. 510.

Turner, Victor W. 1957. *Schism and Continuity in an African Society: A Sturdy of Ndembu Village Life*. Manchester: Manchester University Press.

―――. 1974. *Dramas, Fields and Metaphors*. Ithaca: Cornell University Press.

Vanlandingham, Kenneth E. 1964. "The Decline of the Justice of the Peace." *Kansas Law Review*, 12:389–403. Reprinted in John A. Robertson (ed.), *Rough Justice: Perspectives on Lower Criminal Courts*. Boston: Little, Brown, 1974.

Van Velsen, J. 1967. "The Extended-Case Method and Situational Analysis." In A.L. Epstein (ed.), *The Craft of Social Anthropology*. London: Tavistock.

Varenne, Herve. 1977. *Americans Together: Structured Diversity in a Midwestern Town*. New York: Teachers College Press.

Wagner, Roy. 1981. *The Invention of Culture*. Chicago: University of Chicago Press.

Walzer, Michael. 1963. "Puritanism as a Revolutionary Ideology." *History and Theory*, 3:59–90.

Weber, Max. 1967. In Max Rheinstein (ed.), *On Law in Economy and Society*. New York: Simon and Schuster.

White, James B. 1990. *Justice as Translation*. Chicago: University of Chicago Press.

Wickersham Commission. 1931. "Petty Offenses and Inferior Courts." In *Report on Criminal Procedure*, National Commission on Law Observance and Enforcement, pp. 6–15. Reprinted in John A.

Robertson (ed.), *Rough Justice: Perspectives on Lower Criminal Courts*. Boston: Little, Brown, 1974.

Williams, Raymond. 1977. *Marxism and Literature*. Oxford: Oxford University Press.

Winnicott, D. W. 1971. *Playing and Reality*. London: Tavistock.

Winstanley, Gerrard. 1652. "The Law of Freedom in a Platform; or True Magistracy Restored." In George H. Sabine (ed.), *The Works of Gerrard Winstanley*. New York: Cornell University Press, 1941.

Yngvesson, Barbara. 1976. "Responses to Grievance Behavior: Extended Cases in a Fishing Community." *American Ethnologist*, 3(2):353–373.

———. 1984. "What Is a Dispute About? The Political Interpretation of Social Control." In Donald Black (ed.), *Toward a General Theory of Social Control*, Vol. 2. New York: Academic Press.

———. 1988a. "Disputing Alternatives: Settlement as Science and as Politics." *Law & Social Inquiry*, 13(1):113–132.

———. 1988b. "Making Law at the Doorway: The Clerk, the Court, and the Construction of Community in a New England Town." *Law and Society Review*, 22(3):409–448.

———. 1989. "Inventing Law in Local Settings: Rethinking Popular Legal Culture." *Yale Law Journal*, 98:1689–1709.

———. 1993. "The Meanings of 'Community' in Community Mediation." In Sally E. Merry and Neal Milner (eds.), *Popular Justice*. Ann Arbor: University of Michigan Press.

Yngvesson, Barbara, and Lynn Mather. 1983. "Courts, Moots, and the Disputing Process." In Keith O. Boyum and Lynn Mather (eds.), *Empirical Theories About Courts*. New York: Longman.

INDEX